THE SECRET MANEUVER

A historical crime novella

Elizabeth von Witanovski

ISBN 978-1-956696-53-0 (paperback)
ISBN 978-1-956696-54-7 (hardcover)
ISBN 978-1-956696-55-4 (digital)

Copyright © 2021 by Elizabeth von Witanovski

All rights reserved. No part of this publication may be reproduced, distributed, or transmitted in any form or by any means, including photocopying, recording, or other electronic or mechanical methods without the prior written permission of the publisher. For permission requests, solicit the publisher via the address below.

Rushmore Press LLC
1 800 460 9188
www.rushmorepress.com

Printed in the United States of America

Act well your part; there all the honor lies.

—Alexander Pope

PROLOGUE

"Don't you talk to me like that, sir!"

The index finger shot forward; were it a blade, it would have surely slashed Frederik's face.

Instead, it stopped an inch from his battlefield dust–covered skin, the face belonging to a man of indifferent age—as war evens out all men. Bloodshot narrow, pale eyes; one eyebrow burnt half off; greasy long hussar hair in narrow braids tied in their ends with dirty blue sashes; dry lips under blade-thin mustache measured the rhythm of victory: "I'll talk to you as I choose, for you have no power over me anymore!"

ACT 1

"Did the post coach arrive yet?"

A male voice, still in low range from his afternoon nap—a voice used to command, to be in control—came from behind a sumptuously upholstered tall, old-fashioned backrest.

"Go and look if the flag is up on the mast at Golden Swan."

"As you wish, my lord." Franz, the Count's valet, ran out at once.

Count preferred his household to be small. He surrounded himself with an easygoing, reliable group. His new valet was a clever, agile young man of many skills.

"A new broom sweeps well!" Frau Magdalena Ebner, the housekeeper, giggled the other day.

She loved using her grandmother's tease of newcomers. It brought back memories of her first days here. (She too was then the new broom.) Her speed, combined with her lack of efficiency, drove the old housekeeper crazy. Now she was "our treasure," as her beloved Thomas, the house steward—and a man of many talents like herself—would say. Upon discovering her gift for cooking, she was handed a full load of running the household.

The young Countess was not herself ever since the mysterious death of her husband on the battlefield. It was up to Magdalena to create and oversee the smooth mechanism of everyday life. And quite a responsibility it was with the large family with young children and the patriarch, Count Leopold von Schönbruck, at its helm.

In this noble household, everything ticked like the tall Schwarzwald clock standing in the whitewashed ground-floor corridor. Their townhouse, one of several properties they owned in Austria, was an ancient seat dating back over four centuries.

This noble family had served the Holy Roman emperors time and time again. Their simple titles multiplied and grew in rank and importance. Recently they were able to relax a bit—in fact, all of Europe relaxed and exhaled. General peace took everybody by surprise. As chroniclers will note, "There were no two countries fighting against each other."

Suddenly, there was a breather: people decided to marry, have more children, solve old grudges, let mysteries be gone, and felt compelled to tie loose ends.

The European stage was lit through pink- and yellow-colored filters of permanently happy days, full sunshine with blue skies above.

When they drank—*Prost!*—at this 1801 New Year's midnight, their hopes were high. It was not to last; but they mercifully did not know that yet. They drank their glass to the bottom, disregarding the fact that Napoleon just defeated them at Marengo this past year.

"Whoa, whoa, whoa, prrr!" the coachman's hoarse voice yelled from the high seat. Bending backwards, he skillfully pulled on long reins to halt his fine horses.

He was all bundled up in a pelerine as brown as his eyes. His black felt hat was held down by a yellow scarf, tied across the top, down under his chin, and back to protect his ears. The four groschen, the kind of gray horse with silver spots like small coins on their rear, which gave them their nickname, stopped at once if in slight succession.

The post coach from Vienna had just arrived in Innsbruck. Announcing its arrival at Golden Swan Inn, the flag flew up on the mast.

Passengers who sat up high with the coachman climbed down one man after another. A young woman—her drum-shaped purple hat-box in hand, all bundled up in a vast woolen coat and furs—was carried down like a yellow withered bloom.

The post guard climbed down backward from his place. His muscles were stiff, as he was standing outside the back of the coach, guarding the blue metal mailbox through the long journey. Only now he replaced his earmuffs with a short top hat, then briskly stretched his limbs. Hands in thick leather gloves, he started unhooking belts and chains holding the safety box, the objective of this trip and source of his meager income.

Two pairs of horses—foam at their mouth, loud breath and neigh, their glorious bodies drenched in sweat—tried, to no avail, to derange the flies by whipping their tails, with hair mercilessly cut in half.

"This was not as bad as I thought," said the wife of an imperial judge to her companion inside the thickly upholstered coach.

Her little daughter woke up and whined, but her mother paid no attention. She was focused on her body under her fine muslin petticoats.

I hope it's a boy this time.

She reached for her large lynx-fur muff placed on her companion's knees. "Anneliese?"

It was clear that working hours had just begun. Annelise handed the heavy accessory to her mistress with a weak smile.

The company inside the coach was coming to. These were passengers who could afford to sit in comfort from Vienna all the way to the imperial town of Innsbruck.

I'm sure I know that face!

Quido von Glaubitz, who sat across Madame Judge and who only traveled the last fifteen miles, looked one more time to his right. He never forgot a face.

He turned to the young lady, and, when he caught her eye, suggested, "Did I have the pleasure, madame . . . in Vienna, perhaps?"

She looked him straight in the eye, thinking, *If you mean Burgtheater, then yes.*

Out loud she expressed her regrets, "I don't think it possible, sir."

She then smiled coquettishly, reassuringly. Her face changed; the brightness of her features seemed to put all around her to drab.

Judge's wife noticed first and hurried her small crowd out of the confining space. She never stayed where she wasn't in the spotlight.

Von Glaubitz, the publisher of the *Innsbruck Blatt* newspaper, hit his imaginary forehead.

Why of course! You must be Desiree. Incognito in Innsbruck. I wonder what or who brings you here.

"I hope you'll have a nice time in Innsbruck, madame." He bowed and pressed his brown silk top hat firmly on his salt-and-pepper mane of hair.

"Thank you," said the young woman; her voice was pleasant and bright, trained to project. "I doubt it."

Her eyes stayed in his for one brief moment longer. It was that fraction of a second which only a woman of stage was not shy to do. He felt a rush of blood through his spine; he couldn't remember the last time it felt this exciting. Desiree, that's what she was—desire personified.

She pulled down a fine, expensive blue Italian lace veil over her face and waited until he stepped out from the coach before her.

A bird suddenly hit the windowpane.

"Au! That must have hurt!" noted Leopold. "Was it a swallow?"

His friend glanced through the window.

"A sparrow, I think. Oh yes, and she wore an interesting ring—two birds chasing each other." His index finger suggested the movement around.

Leopold turned toward the window. "They built their nest under the roof this year."

"Who?"

"The swallows."

His friend knew him well.

Leopold Count von Schönbruck listened only when it was about him, his interests, or his experiences.

"The young woman in the post coach I told you about, she wore an interesting ring . . . with birds," Von Glaubitz said without a rush. He was the patient one here.

"A ring with birds?"

"Yes, such a fine spinning thing you don't see every day—two birds chasing after each other . . . in gold."

The Secret Maneuver

Leopold wanted to say "I once bought such a ring for a girl—a kid still,"; but he didn't say a word.

That memory was too awkward. It was one of those gifts to buy a man a clean conscience. He paid more for it than he intended but didn't want to bargain. It was always on his mind that, perhaps, she might sell it for good money at times of need. Perhaps, she did after all.

What was her name? Memory's such a strange sieve.

"Are you all right?" Quido von Glaubitz, full of concern, looked at his old friend. "Should I leave you?"

"No, no, do stay. I must have walked too long today. The market is such a fun place to be before Easter."

He called Franz to bring them something strong to drink.

"Your usual?" he asked Quido.

Quido nodded. "I hope your pain will calm down soon."

When drinks arrived, Leopold drank his right away without saying "Prost!" or "Health!" or anything. His friend didn't stay long after that.

Leopold looked through the crystal glass—clear, with tiny little bubbles caught for posterity in the smooth stem. His thoughts were stirring, trying to reassure him.

It is certainly a coincidence! It has to be a coincidence!

He poured himself one more glass and drank it without tasting the wine's full body, his friend Quido so admired.

Giovanna kept looking around the square. She finally exhaled.

Lucky, she saw him first through the shop window. And then maybe that wasn't him after all.

No, that certainly wasn't him. I only imagined him, she told herself.

She was sure now.

Georg couldn't be that old, she mused. *I wish I could have seen his eyes—the green hue was so unusual, magical. What would he be doing here anyway, this far from Adige? No, it wasn't him.*

5

But her fear didn't abate right away. It was a fear mixed with an undiminished volume of longing she wasn't ready to admit.

Giovanna decided to cross the square and mix into the Saturday market crowd. She preferred to see before being seen. She stepped out of the haberdasher's shop onto freshly swept cobblestones.

Bright early spring sunlight measured up one fine day. All of Innsbruck was in a joyful, festive, colorful mood. She decided not to pull her veil lower over her eyes.

She walked in clouds of a sweet smell of hay; freshly washed granite blocks under her feet were evaporating water and horse pee in a stinking mix. It bothered her, and she pressed her green suede reticule over her short nose.

Giovanna's ears were filled up with shouts of market vendors, the neighing of horses, the shuffle of baskets full of dried fruits and the first bunches of new vegetables, fragrance of the last winter apples stored in straw. She loved every ounce of it all. It wrapped her senses with familiarity which made her smile. She stopped thinking about her fright.

Nonsense. What fright?

With gusto she inhaled clouds of vanilla, cinnamon, ginger, bitter almonds; the sweet smell of honey and lemon and marzipan cookies; the scent of fragrant sugar canes, of freshly baked breads and strudels, their crusts_ a glossy golden rust; a pleasant pinch inside her nostrils from cheeses wrapped in cool large, deep green horseradish leaves.

She had forgotten how much she loved all this, even when it mixed with the smell of livestock pushing through the main street from the next-door square market. That was the real Easter under the Alps!

Something got caught inside her short, black leather boot. She walked in discomfort towards one of the arcades encircling the colorful town square. Leaning her hips on a broad column, plastered in light green, she tried to get rid of the little stone. Noises, smells, and scents—yes, especially those—they were stored in her senses. It all looked and smelled like on the other side of the Alps when she was still a girl. Yes, they never failed her. Her sense of smell was her private museum, her very own archive.

The Secret Maneuver

It must have been sometime in the '80s... oh, those 1780s, her youth...

It was, as usual, quite challenging to be moving the whole troupe of Commedia dell'arte players from one engagement to the other. The carts stuffed with all their possessions were heavy even after everybody jumped out at the heel of the long slope. Now, all the actors were on their feet, walking next to them. One of them was holding a scenery board, sticking out from under the canvas cover. It was a trompe l'oeil—painted trellis of ivy and roses. The piece stood through all comedies and tragedies; one could tell from its ware that it was a rough life. Their most valuable masks_stored in baskets, wrapped in chamois and placed in hay_ were carried by women on their heads.

The horses kept working hard to get the traveling troupe's life up the hill.

"Push!" Marco called to his men, their hands holding to the cart.

He knew them well. They were probably waiting for the horses to pull them along.

"Don't be lazy! Push! Harder!" The slope was long, and they must elevate their four hardworking horses at least a bit. "Forward, forward!"

The troupe—men, women and children—knew him well too. None of them wanted to fall on the wrong side with Marco.

Long minutes on that slope felt like a never-ending treadmill—long enough to bring all sorts of thoughts in anybody's mind, especially Marco's. He'd left his body and soul way back behind him in Italy. She did to him what no other woman ever had before. Only now he felt that going forward was the last thing he wished to happen.

After their success at the ducal court in Venice, then others, in Mantua and Milan in early spring, it was decided that they were ready for Paris. First, they will try their art down here in the south, merely for a week. After that, they will move slowly up north.

Giovanna looked sideways at her father, Marco—statuesque, dark, handsome, and at forty, very much the man whom women found irresistible. Now, Marco was sweaty, his curly head down, heaving, breathless . . . not much of the boastful, loud Spaniard Capitano he's on stage.

There was walking her mother and his wife, Flora Bernini. She was ten years older and the troupe's soul and heart. Theirs was the long family tree of Italian actors of commedia dell'arte. Giovanna knew her family's exciting history by heart. Some of her ancestors went faraway, up to Austria—no, wait, perhaps to Bohemia? They played at Emperor Rudolf's court in Prague! They say that all of them stayed there.

North! One day she'll travel to all of the royal courts of Europe. She'll be the great actress, despite all those who say that the only talent in this troupe is her cousin Gabriel.

All her siblings were dispersed into the world of traveling theatre, some went to the Americas or somewhere else. Giovanna was the youngest.

At fourteen she was a young woman with gifts that all other ladies surely envied. Her hazel eyes had a twinkle over which many a man had lost sleep. She was the young Isabella from the pair of Lovers. Her stage love interest was a man in his thirties. Very handsome. She couldn't stand him.

She gave a sigh, her breasts filling the neckline. It was uncomfortable. Her body tilted towards the hill, her feet not slowing down their effort, as she started undoing the laces on her bodice. Everything that was didn't matter now. Somewhere in front of her was a bright new life.

Finally, the troupe's Principale, the owner and director, Flora Bernini, exclaimed, "Stop!"

They were on the top of the hill, and down, in front of them —France!

The group of actors slowed down, catching their breath. Their eyes turned forward, measuring the vast French countryside in front of them. There, their brilliant future lay ahead.

From that direction, a fashionably ornate postillion with six was slowly making its way up the hill. All the footmen were running alongside, helping to push their master.

When they were about to pass, one of them called in Italian at the troupe of actors, "Turn! Turn! France is out of her mind! My master's rushing back to his estates in Naples."

They all stopped moving in succession as their tired minds couldn't process the words.

Some were still stretching their backs, spreading their arms far in the air above them. Some bent down, hung their head and shoulders to relieve pain. Everybody was breathing heavily. The passing information couldn't quite catch up with them. Was nobody capable of a quick judgement?

"Flora! Say something."

Flora, the reason and brains of this troupe, was standing there, her mind blank.

She turned back towards their homeland they were about to leave; her fists firmly on top of her hips, she looked over the countryside. Roads on both sides were running down the hill—both inviting, both difficult.

"Let's take some rest for an hour or so."

All needed to recuperate, both folks and animals. They pulled off the road under a rock and took down the heavy collars off tired horses to give them some well-deserved rest.

On the side of the rock, there was a narrow path up the hill. A spring of fresh water up there gave this place its name, the Hunter's Swig.

Flora's husband came to sit next to her up there on the grass. He put his arm around his wife's broad shoulders.

"God decided, wouldn't you say, my dove?"

"Don't you 'dove' me! How can God stand such lies!" Flora crossed herself, eyes turned up to heavens as her muffled shout slipped out of her troubled heart. "All you want now is to go back to that whore as quickly as possible."

"Don't talk about her like that! She's our generous supporter."

"Oh yes, she supports you . . . in all positions possible! No! We are sticking to our plan."

"We can easily return from here now."

"Over my dead body! Do you hear?"

"Oh, c'mon. Why all this over nothing! Madame Contessa would—"

"She's a Countess like I am the Queen of Sheba! You are shameless . . ."

The last word was more of a sob. Flora didn't anticipate losing control. She stood up and crossed her woolen scarf tighter across her breasts, already in that angle of her body she was moving away from him.

"Oh, c'mon, dove, let's turn now."

"No! You heard me—over my dead body!"

She ran down the narrow gravel path carefully with the agility of a much younger woman. She never opposed him; she'd been madly in love with him for all those decades. And she hated herself for that!

She still loves me! Marco chuckled. His head stayed turned to her direction, *That's incredible! She truly does.*

He took one more gulp from a small flat flask enveloped in dry grass weave. *Well then, let's see now who has more power here!* Heat from the spirits grabbed his throat. It flooded his brain. He knew that she would do what he wanted; she'd always be on his side, no matter what.

Marco stood up, pushed the flask inside his pocket, and hesitated. His legs felt heavy as he negotiated his way down the little path full of small rocks; pebbles, slippery after the last strong rain, decided to roll with each of his steps.

Once closer to the troupe, he stopped above them on the slope. He wanted to be seen and heard well. His strong legs spread for support, as he would have done on stage. He cleared his throat and took one deep breath.

"Forward! We will go down to Nice! That's settled!" Laura's voice boomed over the heads of her troupe. She looked up at her husband, "Isn't it so, Marco?"

Her raised eyebrows finished the challenge for her, *So what are you going to do now, Maestro?*

Her husband was standing there—his face washed blank, speechless, his anger glued to his face like a mask. When he finally closed his mouth, his jaws pressed hard together. His clenched teeth almost shattered. *This is not going to be!*

Somebody kept shouting "Strudels! Pretzels!" but Giovanna stood motionless like a statue, her short boot still in hand.

She would have loved to know what they talked about up that path. Her father was not a man to be trifled with. She shook her head voluntarily to rid her mind of him.

"Don't think about the past," Giovanna heard her mother's voice, *"Hours too never look back."*

She bent down to put her boot on. Her eyes were brimming with tears. She fished for her handkerchief and dried her eyes. Still in memories, she absentmindedly tucked the white embroidered square in her sleeve. Then she stood up and stomped her foot on the ground. All her skirts and petticoats fell back to their folds. She stood there watching the colorful chaos of the Easter market. Like all other theatre folk, Giovanna too had her superstitions.

She closed her eyes and thought, *If after I open my eyes I see someone in a red shirt, then all my affairs will turn out well.*

But the old town square didn't share any of her anxieties and didn't bother to produce anything red at all.

She turned and said out loud to the first face that happened to be passing her, "What a perfectly boring town."

"We . . . might see . . ."

Quido von Glaubitz was trying to light his meerschaum pipe. It was not going well. He puffed several times to get it going.

"A murder trial . . . we might see . . ." He puffed a few more times. "Here, in Innsbruck."

White circles were slowly floating up.

His pipe was carved into a naive scene with hunting dogs chasing deer all around its circumference; it was tinted to rust hues by years of smoking. He stretched his legs from the floor cushion, straight, forward on the parquetted floor.

I wish you would light your pipe and then talk, thought his friend Leopold.

"A murder trial? Here?" Leopold instead said calmly, glancing back at von Glaubitz in disbelief. "You must be joking."

He too was preoccupied with his meerschaum. But his old friend was serious.

"I am afraid so. A man came into some wealth, now wants his case to be opened, properly looked into."

"After how long?" Count von Schönbruck inquired, finally getting his pipe going.

He inhaled and smiled. He closed his eyes, enjoying their calm little hour.

"Decades, they say." Von Glaubitz manipulated the tapestry cushion back under his cold feet. "I wouldn't have thought."

"Decades?" The fine craftsmanship of Leopold's meerschaum pipe was obviously several classes above his companion's. "Is there any chance that something could be done after such a long time?"

The perfectly proportioned horse had all the decorations expected of an imperial hussar's regiment. The Schönbruck family coat of arms, carved on its saddlebag, didn't leave any space for doubt who was smoking from this fine specimen.

Von Glaubitz was glad to entertain his old friend.

"Good chance, they think. There's a young woman—the fiancée of the murdered—they say, and also her cousin . . . or his cousin? Eh, who knows. The whole family's coming here now to meet with judges." He puffed and closed his eyes. "So here you have it again, money can buy you—"

"Anything," the Count finished his friend's sentence.

They winked at each other and enjoyed silence for the next few moments. Friends for decades, this was their beloved smoking hour.

Wind rattled the opened window. Leopold got up and walked over to close it. Spring was too cold there under the Alps.

"It's worrisome, come to think of it. One hears horrid stories, as if wars weren't enough." He closed the window and turned the brass handle, cast as a rocaille shaped pearl, shut. "I wonder, was it a cold-blooded crime or perhaps a crime of passion?"

"Oh, you romantic! I do have the answer for you—crime of passion, for sure. I mean, my people say so. I believe that most of the murders are done out of passion, wouldn't you say?"

He puffed several times. Again, there was almost absolute quiet, laced with pigeon calls from the roof.

"Poldi? What do you think?"

His friend's face was distant. Quido would have sworn that it turned pale.

"That young woman was truly very pretty," von Glaubitz said very softly, trying to change the subject.

Leopold looked far away over his friend's head.

"Is that what they say? Well then, it's clear, isn't it? Her fiancé couldn't stand another man's attention and"—Leopold's hand suggested a thrust of a sword forward—"How perfectly romantic."

But his eyes were not present.

"No. I mean, the young woman in the coach, Poldi. She was very pretty, the one in the post coach from Vienna."

"From Vienna?"

"You were not listening!"

"I've been nothing but all attention!"

"I know, I know," Quido rushed in, smoothing out their afternoon.

Leopold looked at him sharply. Quido von Glaubitz played the only card possible.

"I am sorry."

Count thought for a moment, then put his meerschaum back in his mouth and revived it.

He exhaled smoke and chuckled, "Schiller could turn the case into one of his dramas."

The social order was again reestablished in this room; their conversation could continue.

The sun found a long crevice in the tall clouds; without any obstacle in its way, it inundated the whole room with pleasant hues of warm ocher. Quido relaxed; he was finally smoking again. This was one of the perfect moments he so cherished—silence, filled up with friendship.

"You know, I think I recognize her. I'm sure she's an actress," he smiled at Leopold.

Leopold swallowed smoke and started coughing.

Back to Vienna then. Giovanna looked into the tall psyche mirror standing by the heavy oak door.

She was all packed. Her bag, her hat box, and her traveling trunk—she packed light this time. She didn't have any social obligations there. The small group of her luggage had to be moved down to the postillion.

She spun the revolving drum-like platform with concealed drawers. What remained was to fix her fashionable turban before porters came. She'd cached her fine hatpins in there yesterday. She looked up in the oval looking glass, tilted on the angle to show the top of one's head.

The long fancy hatpin—with a large, oval, red coral bead—was pinned from the right, just above her forehead, into her cream woolen turban. The second one, with simply polished carnelian, was inserted from the left, in the back, above her nape.

She pulled the mirror down; it gave several dull, muffled bounces, overcoming the carved dents of the central stem. Under the little revolving table, the leg was shaped into a baluster anchored in a softly carved disc standing on three small wooden balls. Beautiful piece in rosewood.

Giovanna smiled. The inn she visited was fine and comfortable. Her career was in full swing—she could afford little indulgences now. When the new theatre season opens, she would be on stage every night. She was in all of Shakespeare: she's Juliet, she's Catherine, she's Cleopatra.

But she will be also coming back there, to the Innsbruck Court Theatre, to do some classics, to show off her craft. Her performance as Juliet was deemed especially fine. Next summer taken care of, she felt good about herself like never before. Her smile warmed up her face. She needed another reason to come here than the solicited meeting with her estranged father. Her fingers touched the contract, placed safely in the green suede reticule. A small golden bird got caught in its embroidery.

She was invited to Innsbruck, to give testimony at the judicial court. But what testimony?

Her fingers were carefully untangling her favorite ring from the web of silk threads. Giovanna had feared meeting her father after all those years. She'd heard that he'd been living somewhere in Italy.

That he left people to their destiny after dissolving the commedia troupe of Mother's. *Typical*, Giovanna thought.

She rather hoped that he had no idea who or where she was. She was wrong. Now he was able to buy the memory of people he tossed overboard. Maybe theirs; they need money. Not hers!

Giovanna's grudge had never ceased. In her eyes, he was the guilty one.

Now he dares to open this case. *Money!* He surely hopes to make more out of it. Blackmail was never too foreign a word to him.

She pulled harder, and the golden bird cut one of the silk threads.

"Damn! And damn him again!" She lost her patience. "Where are the servants?"

She was getting too warm. Giovanna unhooked her overcoat and took down the fox shawl.

She stood up and walked to the window, opened it, and shouted down, "I have been waiting up here forever!"

With a quick set of brief, light knocks, a maid opened the door. "Madame called?"

"I've been packed for hours! Send the porters here now!"

Quick, quick, quick! Let's hurry away from here! She didn't want to remember any of it, at all.

Cold shiver in one particular spot reminded her of her constrained nerves. On the left, in the middle by her spine, it always tingles painfully. Or was it the sudden cold breeze? Giovanna crossed to the window and shut it.

Noisy steps of two robust men grew in volume. They walked in, murmuring something close to "grüss gott"; then all was moving out and towards future: the shuffle of the trunk on wooden planks, her quick "I'll carry my hatbox myself" and noises on the stairs, men negotiating the curve of the steep staircase, and their voices moving outdoors.

The postillion coach was being packed up high. Thick leather belts fixed the travel trunks to the roof. The tempo of the servants running in and out of the inn resembled quite unpleasantly the speed of her thoughts.

Swallows were busy building their new nest in the stable, their black-and-white bodies flickered through the air back and forth full of spring energy.

Giovanna looked down at her ring. She will not give her father any satisfaction. She will not name the man who killed Gabriel because . . .

She turned abruptly from the window towards her empty room.

"Because, Your Honor—oh, it's so embarrassing, but I don't remember. I cannot recall anything. It was such a long time ago, as Your Honor would agree. I was practically a child. You see, I'd simply forgotten."

Her speech was loud and clear as if in front of Innsbruck judges again.

A few moments later, her low heels tapped resolutely on the wooden boards. She rushed down the solid dark, ox-blood-stained oakwood stairs and didn't look back.

Quido von Glaubitz started towards his usual place at the alcove. Innsbruck was all prepared for Easter. Freshly washed windows glared in still-scarce sunlight. Squares and streets were swept, new skirts bought and fitted, and Easter breads baked.

His friend Leopold was already sitting, puffing away when he arrived with his Thursday news. Before sitting down in his usual chair, he took out something from his pocket and stepped back towards Leopold.

"Ah, I have here"—he stretched his arm and waved a small white square of cloth in front of Leopold's nose—"a lovely fine little thing."

"What is it?" Count moved his head back, trying to escape the unknown piece.

"I found it on the street the other day; and with no one around to claim it, I kept it."

Leopold looked at his old friend. "You? You found it?"

"Why? What's wrong with me finding—"

"Now, now, I know about several women—some married, even, and, worse, some engaged—who would gladly give you their handkerchief only if you promised to wear it close to your heart."

Quido laughed the laugh of pleasure and agreeable flattery.

"Yes!" He gave a nod and extended his hand and dropped the white cloth into Leopold's lap. "But no, not this one. I found it by an arcade column."

Leopold placed his meerschaum in a cherrywood pipe holder, then carefully lifted the fine, delicate piece of fabric. He recognized it immediately.

"Nice, isn't it?" Quido took it from him, lifting it to his nose. "And it's lightly perfumed. Here, tell me what you'd say this is? I thought sort of a rose or verbena, isn't it?"

He waved the handkerchief in front of Leopold again.

"Oh, I don't know. I don't feel like sniffing some . . . some . . ."

"Oh, and I meant to tell you that trial is on its way. The rich man—his name was so Italian—something, something Bernini_"

Leopold stood up so suddenly that his arm hit the pipe holder. It fell, and one of his meerschaums broke

"Damn!"

"Poldi! What got into you?" Quido knelt down to help his friend pick up the pieces. "You are in a bad mood today, my friend."

"I'm sorry, recently I don't feel well." Leopold stood up and rang the small bell.

Franz came in. He saw the mess.

Leopold handed him the few pieces he picked up. "Look into this."

His servant tactfully omitted any questions and left.

Leopold touched Quido's arm and said, "I am sorry."

"That's all right, that's all right. Don't worry about it. Go, have some rest. We'll have our little hour next week."

Von Gloubitz's hand probed the outside of his black woolen overcoat. His palm recognized the shape of his pipe. It was one of his mannerisms to make sure that his meerschaum waits for him in the deep pocket.

"All will be well again!"

Before his friend could have become too embarrassed about their conversation, he picked up his walking stick, placed his top hat provocatively on a slant, and left the smoking room.

Von Gloubitz's "Till the next week!" came already from the main staircase.

Just as he started walking down, there was Franz coming with a broom and a sweeping pan. Quido's head was full of questions as the recurrence of his friend's changed behavior made him rethink their conversations.

He looked at the servant and asked, "Is my friend all right?"

Shrugged shoulders was the only answer he got as this household is a lip-tied, discrete entity.

The postillion coach was shaking on the cobblestones. Giovanna's body, comfortably pressed towards the dark green cushions in her corner, kept swaying with the rhythm of the springs.

She closed her eyes the moment she exchanged smiles with a rich burgher's wife sitting opposite her. There was a conversation waiting in that face_ a long, dull one.

Giovanna had her very own to attend to. Still the one with her father centerstage. Her mind was unable to get rid of it. She agreed to come here because she'd craved to see her father's face when he heard her decision. She wasn't ready to indulge him, to bring possible turmoil to her own life.

Her naivete, as he knew it, stayed back in Italy on the wobbly stage of her family traveling troupe.

Father—his wealthy Italian Contessa had changed him—now was all about money. Contessa had bequeathed to him everything she possessed. He's got all of her fortune; he has enough to call law to his side if he decides.

She remembered all his little tricks, his little thefts, the crying women, begging men, she shook her head in disgust. His money. No, she would not testify in his case. Not for him. She will always recall his face. Priceless. Was he furious beside himself! Giovanna felt victorious. Money cannot buy you everything.

No. She shouldn't have come here. She lost one of her precious mementos.

Her mind flew freely as the postillion picked up speed once they paid the toll at the town's gate.

Giovanna was still young; regardless of what she noticed in that looking glass that morning—new tiny wrinkles around her eyes.

She knew well how those two deep lines between her eyebrows have been deepened time and time again. At times more, at others less, satisfying. She never believed in controlling her face when smiling and even less when lovemaking. One day, when those two wrinkles vanish, her youth will be definitely gone.

She's had her mother's blood. She fell in love easily without thinking. She was able to be in love with two, even three, men at the same time. Deeply in love. Equally with them all. Inexplicably. Uncomfortably at times.

She loved her men with every nuance there was,—suffering jealousy when they turned after a woman, defending them passionately had the occasion arisen, working to bits if they were in need. No, nobody has ever been able to understand that. And yet, sometimes a man was there only to please her. She would walk away without ever remembering his name again.

She was very lucky in that. Only a few centuries ago, some of her lovers, feeling betrayed by her acting like any man around, would have surely dragged her to stake, to burn her as a witch. Lucky for her, 1801 belonged to modern times.

When Quido von Glaubitz returned to Leopold's house the following week, the old footman had a message for him: "Herr Count sends his apologies. His Grace left for his hunting lodge for the season. Do visit him as you wish."

Von Glaubitz stood there, surprised. The old footman knew him well.

"Would you care to come in and have some wine, sir?"

Quido was puzzled. *Season? He never goes before June.* He moved his bamboo walking stick with a cobalt knob to his left hand. "No, no thank you. I will get in touch with him."

Leopold was his lifelong friend; he knew all about him.

Season? Maybe Leopold's getting old. At fifty-two? Are you mad?

The servant was waiting at the open gate just in case his master's friend changed his mind. But he did not.

I'll visit him up there. That's what I'm going to do, right away! Quido von Glaubitz started walking back towards his offices on Saint Johann's Square. He knew himself too well. If it hasn't concerned his work, the "right away" was not in his vocabulary.

ACT II

His body jerked with such force that Count von Schönbruck woke up. His heartbeat, which was about to shatter his throat, echoed painfully up to his head.

He covered his ears. That didn't help.

He glanced around, still in the cool veil of midday sleep. There was his book down on the Persian carpet, spread like an exotic bloom. He hated dreams—time which he had no control of like his guilt, his fear. There was nowhere to hide. The embroidered handkerchief was in their center.

Why now? Why is this all happening now? It was just an episode, a long gone sore.

He saw a pretty girl, almost a child, and fell for her. He knew from the start it was all just a pass-through, just an adventure.

He was already engaged; he loved his fiancée. Although the match was arranged by their families, they were in luck—it was love at first sight. Leopold would have never betrayed her.

That little young actress was like a candy—that was all. She was delicious. His senses got flooded by her presence. He desired to breathe her, to be around her days and nights. But in the end, he didn't mean anything serious. It was a play, an exciting game.

She must have surely known; she's the traveling comedians' daughter, for God's sake!

He heard his friend Quido the way he looked at him when he said, "Memory is a dwelling set upon a fluid base with secret chambers locked by fears."

What did he mean by that?

Leopold looked at the book on the carpet: crushed, its old binding loosened; some of the frail pages, the color of thinly brewed tea, fanned disorderly out. Leopold was irritated by his sudden feeling of responsibility and guilt.

He reached for the volume, Rousseau, he smuggled when he had to return from France in 1783—now an injured friend. *My fault!* He was so young then. He felt no connection to that young man at all.

Leopold was able to reach the book easily from his low armchair—broad, heavily upholstered—a unique specimen from the century of his youth. It was fondly christened 'a hippo' by his grandchildren.

"Grandfather?" said a little girl's voice and concluded his selfish hour.

He made an effort to smile and sit up straight.

"Louisa, and how are you, my little dear?"

His eldest granddaughter smiled broadly in place of her answer—her typical self. She stood in the tall library doorway, her translucent white dress meandering forward, pushed by the breeze from behind. Doors and windows were opened throughout the whole hunting lodge at this time of year.

"Are you not going to kiss your Opa?"

She must have been holding her breath ever since she entered the library, for now she exhaled out loud and briskly crossed the space with a double skip.

Louisa kissed her grandfather Leopold's powdered cheek. She smiled, her small, short nose still on his skin. How she loved kissing him! The inimitable scent of quince felt like a protective eiderdown. Her kiss always cued grandpa to say things like "There, now my morning is complete."

His pleasant, closely shaven face lit up from within. He asked what he could do for his darling. She was hesitant and was not ready to talk.

The Count enjoyed this prolonged moment of intimacy: Louisa in the morning light coming through the new tall windows, Louisa in her translucent morning-white gauze dress, her broad fine pantaloons, morning light playing on her simple blue hemp with green dots slippers, a small nosegay of June flowers in her deep neckline.

She was smaller than other girls of her just recently celebrated twelve years but by far smarter than much older young ladies who would come to call at their townhouse in Innsbruck or stopped up here just for a day of hiking.

Louisa made a step forward, but then, instead of choosing his thigh—which has been the usual spot for their talks—she turned her back to him and slid down on his footrest.

She leaned against his shin; *a good sign,* he thought.

The footrest was covered in kilim, a small carpet the Count had brought back from his trip to Anatolia. It was woven of itchy colorful wool. At any other time, Louisa would have tucked her shawl under her, but she didn't notice today.

"Opa, what exactly Mama means when she says that I have 'vivid ima. . .'?" Louisa hesitated.

That was a new word in this household. Count was curious. "Vivid imagination?"

"Yes, vivid imagination," said Louisa carefully with her usual ambition to master the unknown right away. "What does she mean?"

"She means that…that you are a bright, intelligent girl who is creative and can deduce facts quicker than any other girl!" he concluded with his usual creativity.

Louisa turned up and looked into the deep pool of his green eyes as he bent down towards her.

"That's not exactly what she means, right?"

He sat back and said, "See, right now you are being more clever than the rest."

Count von Schönbruck kissed his granddaughter's not-so-neatly combed short hair à la Titus and looked out the window. Gray clouds over the Alps were way back but rapidly moving forward.

"Clouds o'r Saint Ann, bring down the rain," is that how it goes?
"Grandpa?"

"I'm listening. Your mother also means that you have the rare ability to grasp situations to see deep into people's souls and sometimes—well, you know I think you simply . . ."

He was carefully looking for a word.

"She doesn't believe me? Is that it?" Her voice was an octave higher now. "Right?"

She stood up so abruptly that it made her blush. She'd never felt such anger with her mother before.

Louisa immediately collected herself.

"I am sorry, Opapa." Without planting her usual kiss on his cheek she rushed out to the corridor.

Leopold turned his head after her.

Opapa? Is she slipping into difficult years already? She doesn't look like she would, the Count feared.

"Opa," Louisa's head appeared sideways in the doorway, "I'm so glad you came here sooner this year. It's been such a sweet month already, Opa."

She gave him one of her loveliest smiles.

Her scent of rosewater, like silk ribbons from her dress, slid around the polished oak door frame. In a few moments, he heard his beloved little girl laughing outside.

He gave a sigh. His hopes that moving up there in early summer would erase all the other world, didn't happen. He believed in his summer routine of hours with his favorite book and his morning nap. It failed him. This unexpected moment in his life proved to be far more complex than he was ready to admit.

Leopold sat back into the armchair. His knees hurt today; yesterday, he spent all day in the saddle, hunting.

Count reached for a small cowbell, one of his eccentricities the little kids loved.

"My lord?" Johann, his old man, appeared with a slight bow.

He was not in his livery up here in the mountains; instead, he wore a green and brown leather hunting outfit.

"I'll have some herbs, Johann, to help me digest."

Count's old servant bowed again and turned. Only then his smile stretched from one bushy gray sideburn to the other. He knew well by now which herbs the Count had in mind. These were hard times all around them; some things made all that chaos much easier to cope with.

"And I am going to be a hussar!" said the little boy, his wooden toy horse between his thighs, keeping his chin up.

"No! I am going to be a hussar! You can't be a hussar. You don't have a real horse! You are a peon!"

The young boy of about fourteen turned sharply to walk away but then stopped and yelled with reborn anger at his companion.

"You are nobody! You don't have four houses like we have and a palace in Vienna! You can't be a hussar! It's Only I who can!"

"And my brother says you are stupid! And not even your dog likes you!" the other boy standing up to his knees in the grass shouted bravely.

"My Duchess loves me! She's the best dog! You never can have such an expensive dog! You . . . pauper!"

"You stork! Your legs are thin and funny!"

It came out a little harsher than the boy wanted.

"Frederik." He shrugged his shoulders. "I'm sorry . . . I meant—"

"Get out of my sight you little…"

Frederik, the young Count von Schönbruck was looking for the right, strong word. His face was frowning, and then the worst insult he was looking for popped in his head.

"You little baronet!" he shouted with relief.

Frederik turned and started pacing loudly away from that Baron Nobody! That von Who-Knows-Where.

He was stomping his feet as hard as he could and laughing in hiccup-like chains of glory. His black leather boots were crushing bright white river rocks of the perfectly raked path, shooting them away in all directions.

He suddenly stopped, bent down, and gathered all larger river rocks he could find to throw at his opponent. But when he stood up, the boy—his white horse under his armpit—was already too far.

Frederik had no energy to run after him in this heat. He opened his palms and let the stones drop back on the ground in front of him. The river rocks made a pile that looked like a mole's heap or it could be . . .

"A mountain!" Louisa squatted down later that afternoon.

Her perspective changed—here was her new make-believe world! She must show Fred when she finds him. Brilliant! She stood up and picked a small, pointed rock.

She pressed hard on the ground and circled around the heap, proclaiming, "Robinson's Island!"

Fred appeared from nowhere; he heard her idea and stepped on the line she just drew.

His right heel, still in the riding boot, turned into a tool, deepening the line.

"It's a moat, and that's my castle!"

"No, it's Robinson's Island, and it's mine."

"I built it."

"You did not. It was just a heap. I found it."

"You both are too old to play such a silly game," said their mother's melodious voice from the saddle above them.

How did she manage this? She would always appear in the most unexpected moments! The siblings were confused yet impressed.

"Come inside, I need to talk to you."

She was sitting very upright and sideways in the ladies' saddle of pale yellow and red.

Her white thoroughbred made a bright backdrop for her riding clothes—the double-breasted black cotton spencer jacket with silver buttons; a simple gray-blue silk dress; a long, gray silk bobbinet veil, wrapped around her short top hat's crown, was falling long and unadorned to the back, her bespoke pale-blue suede gloves were made short to allow the blue gray Flanders laces to grace her wrists.

Louisa admired her mother's elegance, even though her fashions were still kept in mourning colors. She turned and ran home without turning back at Frederik.

"I meant both of you," stressed his mother's voice sternly, with a question mark in her voice.

She poked her horse with an elegant silver-inlaid, ebony handwhip. The slight animal with meticulously braided hair hopped forward to his first trot. Frederik, her oldest, decided to hear and to obey—for this once.

A rusty hunting dog heeled and sat down, his brown eyes glued to his master's face, to eyes that had always a friendly green glow for him. Count pulled on the intricately woven, flat golden chain. His large pocket watch, oak leaves and acorns engraved on its cover, slipped out into his palm. It was a key-wound timepiece—his prized possession, the one present he'd received from his late father. That was the bittersweet memento of his disciplinarian, elusive father's last day.

He held the watch to his ear under the brown brim of his suede hat. The ticking of this hunting watch was always reassuring. Leopold tucked it back to the small pocket inside the deerskin jacket.

I must speed up!

Prinz, his Irish setter, as always, seemed to agree.

Leopold's schedule was sacred to him. His fingers finally managed to get the small horn button into the stiff leather hole. Prickly pain changed his face to a grimace, one constant reminder of the last battle he took part in. A French hussar's saber scraped him to the bone but most of the two fingers stayed on.

Lucky. Left hand. Could have been much worse.

"True soldier, through and through," you would say about the Count. But you would be wrong.

Prinz's long pink tongue hung from the side of his elegant slim jaw, swaying as he started picking up the speed of his master. The river rock path twined around the hunting lodge and connected in the back with three other paths, each leading to an adjacent service building. Grass and shrubs all around, and further in the park, ancient trees give shade to brooks and a quick river.

Far in front of him, he saw his grandson.

Frederik stood there, idling; his pale eyes narrowed; his lower jaw pushed forward.

"He's wrong!" he said angrily out loud.

Then his anger overwhelmed him, and he started shouting, tears running down his cheeks.

"Duchess loves me! She adores me! She's the best dog! She loves only me!" young Fredrik shouted.

In the middle of the grass meadow, a girl sat up.

"Now, Fred, really. Of course she loves you, and I love you too."

Since she didn't receive any answer, Louisa stood up. Her brother was looking down, his arms hugging his strongly built young body. She wanted him in a good mood.

"Stop being silly. Florian comes here to play with you."

But her brother's lower lip protruded even further forward. There was only one ace to play.

"Let's go and catch trout up in the brook!"

She walked up to him and stretched her suntanned arm; her small palm opened, waiting.

"Come, Fred. We'll catch them in our bare hands!"

It worked. Frederik smiled and grabbed her hand.

"Come you, and bring your Robinson."

He pulled her to the full run.

"There's nothing we can't do!"

This pale little girl was his best friend—for most of the time, anyway.

One hose of his blue pantaloons rolled up, one flimsily slapping his left ankle, they started running up the slope. His boots gave them ideal traction; they were up by the stream in no time.

Louisa's bare feet stepped into the stream.

"Ah, cold!" she giggled and turned back. "Take off your boots, Fred! Come!"

"Never!" called her brother and hopped in the cold water as he was, in his new riding boots.

Oh, Fred!

Count saw his grandchildren running away and shook his head. *Kids.*

He cherished their freedom, something he himself had never had while growing up.

He should have been feeling happy; instead, the slight tingle of fear returned uninvited. He didn't like the idea of fear. He used to drown his own in a bottomless glass of something strong before each battle.

"Get your nine inches of fear out of your soul!" his squire would shout through clouds of tobacco smoke at other soldiers before each battle.

A French sword decapitated him in front of Leopold, and he couldn't save him. The secret maneuver was only Leopold's to have. Only him to protect. Him and all the male descendants of his family.

The letter about his son's death was still too puzzling, "Killed in a sword fight on the battlefield."

That could not be right. They must have made a mistake. The secret maneuver had never failed.

He was certain that his son knew the maneuver well. He himself taught him every nuance, every possibility of when and how to use it. Did his son drink too much before that battle? Probably. Would that explain his death? No. The family secret was deadly, that was that.

The Count's setter was panting, pink tongue bouncing in the corner of his long jaw. They were almost home. Across the large, green space, he could see the hunting lodge. He felt pride every time he looked at the solid, whitewashed walls grounded in thick granite. More of a castle, a keep. Unlike the fragile, elegant chateau his son planned to build in its place—his late son.

Something must have gone wrong. He never understood. He is obliged to teach the maneuver to Frederik. But is the boy mature enough? Will he ever be? Will he mature suddenly as quickly as his father did? Ready at eighteen to tackle the world?

A new wave of sorrow hollowed the space under Count's ribs. He gasped for more air; it sounded like the glissando of his treasured viola. He wiped his wet cheeks with the back of his mutilated hand. That dream, too, vanished in the last battle.

"Early June and already this hot!" Magdalena Ebner untied the wide ribbons of her starched white cotton cap to dry up her forehead. She leaned backwards against the broad cherrywood worktable.

Every single one of the six small windows and both blue painted doors were hooked open to let some air in.

Magdalena shook out her red cotton scarf and decided not to put it back over her shoulders. She stood there, playing with the square of red fabric. She felt unusually short of breath and looked around.

Is it the weather that makes me this hot? Am I getting older? Better not to think that.

She still hoped for her own children, no matter how dangerous, they say, it might be in her age. Thirty-seven years old, not young. Some of her old girl-friends lay under a tombstone. Magdalena crossed herself.

She tossed the red scarf over the chair. Without looking, her strong hand reached for the favorite butcher's knife—but it wasn't there.

Magdalena, Frau Ebner turned all around—it was nowhere to be seen. She turned towards the working table and opened one of the drawers where she kept the sharpening steel. No, she didn't drop it there. Then she peered in the other drawer, the deep one, where bread and rolls were stored. But not there either. She walked towards the door to call her kitchen help Clara whom she gave that particular responsibility of looking after knives and kitchen hatchets.

She needed to summon her there and make the full-breasted short redhead recount all the knives—and out loud, at that. But her idea remained just a thought. Before she could get around to acting on it, the lady's maid walked in unexpectedly with another special request from the young Countess.

The statuesque housekeeper's rare free hour galloped away into another direction. She rolled her eyes up to the heavens.

Some days...really.

With ribbons tightly fixed back under her chin, she led the way to the pantry. As mistress of provisions, she had that chamber under her jurisdiction as well. When she reached for the key on her chatelaine, the cold touch reminded her of the misplaced knife. She envisioned the recount, the questioning, the tears—her mood turned even more drab.

Sharp contours of the Alps all around had gray caps of clouds. Leopold knew that rain would come sometime in the evening. Magdalena told him so; her knees never lie.

He entered the gunroom first and put his weapon carefully on the cleaning table. It was a masterpiece in its category, with brass and mother-of-pearl inlays. He didn't have to tell his men "I will take care of it later myself," but he did anyway.

He turned to his four-legged friend with the last command of their hike, "Stay!"

Then to his men, with a reminder, "Give him water and don't forget he likes gizzards above all."

Count walked to his dog, gave him several friendly "good boy" pats as he was leaving. He turned again by the opened door and ordered,

"And wipe him before he goes back to zwinger, among the others,"

Count went to his quarters to take a bath.

It was seen as eccentric by all. He was the true man of the Age of Enlightenment. He lounged in the bathtub, lined with soft white Turkish cloth, and stayed even after water started cooling down. On a day like this, he didn't mind; he didn't want to be disturbed by hands coming in with more hot water either. No water tap in this old lodge up there.

His eyes closed for complete privacy. He sat there but couldn't relax.

A new scent, when he first stepped in the bath, had brought back such ache.

Did old Johann forget? No citruses!

His late wife's favorite . . . Her scented skin...all night long bathing in her scent. . . lemon. . .their walks in orchards and lemon groves.

She was his first and only real love. He turned mad after she was gone. He made sure that there remained nothing around him from their brief happy life—nothing that could remind him of times they coexisted in such outstanding accord.

Nothing at all! It was all his fault. He couldn't wait to be a father. She died in childbirth. Their first baby and only son.

Leopold took care of everything_He sent away most of her possessions. Her fashions, fans, hairpins, paintings; jewels he sent to the archbishop to be used for a new monstrance. He sold her horse, had her garden replanted, and yet . . .

Broad cheeks flushed with anxiety, Leopold stood up. Waterdrops started running the length of his naked body, sliding and falling back to the bathtub. He was standing there, motionless— his body of a classical sculpture, muscular, impressive in its built; his skin turned dark amber in places where strong mountain sun could freely reach, an olive tint elsewhere; his hair down to his shoulders with only a few gray streaks around his temples.

Johann, his old servant, brought him favorite bath towel. They've known each other well. His old eyes asked, *Why is his lordship so touchy? Who disobeyed this time?*

Leopold, Count von Schönbruck, was drying himself in silence. He suddenly noticed Johann. His old man seemed somewhat shorter today.

He got more frail since he was sick last winter, observed Count. *Time to send him back to town, to retire.*

Leopold picked up speed. He was dressing hurriedly now, wrapping his cravat around his neck with such impatience that he almost stabbed himself with the long golden pin of elk teeth,

"I am not hungry anymore, Johann."

He took out the pin and pressed it in the old servant's shriveled hand. "No lemon scent next time."

Here, Johann had his answer. Before he could say anything apologetic his lord sent him away,

"Bring me a jug of our Tokaji and a slice of bread."

Short time afterwards, his white shirt opened down to his navel; bare feet on the embroidered footrest, Leopold was absentmindedly chewing on thick cuts of speck. He carved them skillfully with one hand holding the knife by its blade. His dark fingers played with small cuts of bread between each bite.

He must go away. There was a disturbing image tucked in the back of his mind. It has been there, kept undisturbed for decades. That has changed. It would come in different times of the day recently, more and more often. He couldn't take the risk. He had a family to think of.

Leopold picked up the crystal glass, full of amber liquid, and looked through its tint. It was magic—even the most overcast day turned into sunlit splendor by an amber filter. It failed to amuse him today.

Just as Frau Ebner's knees had predicted, it was pouring.

The next morning, Count woke up to the sound of heavy raindrops hitting parapets of four small windows of his bedroom. He turned on his side and reached for one of the fine goose-feather dust pillows piled by the headboard. He tucked it under his head and tossed his white cotton night cap on the floor.

Too warm.

He decided to stay in bed longer than on any other morning. He didn't call his old Johann to come and help him dress. When he finally stepped on the honey color of the wooden parquets, their soft, cool touch pleased him all over again. He looked in the small round psyche mirror standing by his bed. There was his face—the face of the man he'd become over decades.

Leopold liked what he was looking at—a good, strong human being: reliable, fine, trustworthy, cultured, and educated. Above all a man known as the highly honorable nobleman to all.

His satisfaction lasted only for so long till swallows flickered past his window. His mind was back in Innsbruck. Unsettling memory of a young actress came frightfully back. But he neither had guts nor honesty to revise the portrait he found in his looking glass at his first uncomplicated glance of mind still foggy from the deep sleep. He hit the psyche's frame. It spun one and half round and stopped with an angry squeal.

It was raining. Giovanna pulled her chair closer to the window. She'd been listening to the beat of drops on the roof for the last few hours.

A little book of poems stayed open in her hand all that time, but she was not reading. Innsbruck was covered in gray mist, all its glossy cobblestones beaten by steady ropes of rain.

The Alps stayed invisible; hidden safely behind thick gray curtains pulled down low over the River Inn and this imperial town. They had no reason to participate in human dramas.

Giovanna was glad this wasn't a day of her theatre performance. She felt tired, without enthusiasm. She will see her father at the judge's office tomorrow. That performance was of a different kind. They didn't part on the jolliest of notes. It took all her self-discipline to remain civil around him.

She'd never forgotten how he behaved after her mother's death: The swift funeral in some small town on the border. The brisk change of plans. He had carts turned, and back to Italy they went.

Why on earth did I answer his letter?

Her curiosity, that's why. "Curiosity killed the cat," her mother would say.

Her reasonable, intelligent mother—agile, at that. Would she walk so dangerously close to the edge of that rock at Sainte Agnés? Giovanna's eyes welled up with helpless tears.

It made her sick when she remembered father opening mother's dead fingers. When they found her she was clutching the golden locket, her family heirloom. She had worn it all her life since her christening. She promised to Giovanna to give it to her on her eighteenth birthday.

Father slipped the jewel in his pocket, and that was it. She was sure it went around his mistress Principessa's neck. She too is gone now. Cholera. The epidemic prevented his father from taking them to Venice. Instead, they went up north to Como, to Adige.

Giovanna moved her ring around her finger. Golden swallows started chasing each other. Georg—her first, true love and her last—there has never been anyone like that, her happiest and the most dreadful memory.

She kissed the ring he gave her; warmth of her own skin brought up long lost emotions. The unexpected wave came so strong that she couldn't stand the confining walls of her room. She put on her pelerine to walk out in the rain. Sudden thunder shook the square outside and rattled the window panes.

Giovanna quickly walked to the small, round table and lit the prepared Saint Medard's candle.

It rained for days. Riverbanks could hardly contain all the water coming down from the hills. The river was like a strong, unleashed beast. You could hear it up in the lodge on a day like this. In calmer times, washerwomen could bring baskets of laundry down to the sparkling-clean stream; stablemen took horses to water them there to cool down their dusty, sweaty bodies after working in fields all day.

They would lead them to the deep and swim, propped on the animals by holding tight their bare sides with strong thighs. Women would come, just to watch, to sing, to look upon their future.

Thunder suddenly rattled the windows. Children playing somewhere in one of the anterooms screamed. Louisa was determined to get through a piece of music. Count heard them all at once—the dissonance, their fright, and voices consoling them.

Rain was beating the long, narrow window panes. The landscape behind them was smudged, the whole valley turned gray, out of reach. Leopold picked up the book he had carefully chosen the day before. It was still his habit to read out loud. The possibility of reading silently felt too new, very foreign, to him.

He loved his own voice. The room becomes alive with the story, its characters, noises, colors, fashions, means of transportation—everything! Every detail is with him and around him, vividly, truly, with scents and smells even.

Why would he refrain from such pleasure?

He loved that feeling of his own involvement, of standing right inside the story, following its flow from within! He wasn't prepared to trade such wealth of feelings for some novelties.

Besides, reading out loud makes him feel his own person. Greeks would call their theatre mask *persona*; so there, *personare*, sounding through that's what he loves to do—to be inside his voice, to hear the sound, to submerge his mind into it; to become one with the characters; to live in the center of the story for those precious moments.

Silent reading! No, that's not for me.

He pulled the chair close to the window. Rain was coming down steadily, but the skies were already lit up from above by summer sunlight. He looked down at his book. *Such a good light for reading!* This was the only time he was glad that his late son pushed for these tall, modern French doors. *Splendid.*

Count's long fingers slid along the red Morocco leather bookmark. Left palm felt the leather front cover. His family coat of arms was embossed in gold, as it was on covers of most of his books.

He carefully lifted the frontispiece and pressed it gently down to the left to make it stay open; the strong scent of paper permeated into his whole face. Count stopped for a second and closed his eyes, just like he would have done when washing his face under the cold stream of waterfall, up in the hill.

He stayed motionless for that initial moment. He observed as the existence of sounds and noises around him subdued; only then he cleared his throat and his eyes were able to see the first word. His voice of baritone timber started filling up the vast tall room; wood-carved lions, sitting on finials of bookshelves' columns, seemed to close their eyes too to listen.

A word. The way he said it. The whole room around Leopold collapsed under its echo. It was not a simple memory but a complex, beautiful, cruel, and intense thought colored in deep hues. Why now? Why his late wife's voice? Why her scent? Count put down the book and as he was, in his soft house jacket, walked out into the pouring rain.

"I cannot promise anything," said the front-chamber official of Innsbruck's judicial court to the small group. "Herr Judge will let you know soon."

This was a precursor to his tossing the case to the waste bin, but they didn't know that.

They turned away with hesitation of people unfamiliar with such gilded spaces; they were intimidated by the vast rooms; countless tall, gilded doors; parquets laid with Persian carpets; gilded chandeliers glittering with crystal icicles; the two enormous paintings of the Emperor and Empress."

They sort of leaned toward each other under the weight of impressions.

It was their trade to play emotions, but this was not their stage; they didn't know how to deal with this. They seemed to be squeezed together even, without touching, the way they used to be in their canvas covered cart in cold weather years ago.

They used to be a good troupe; they would perform in towns on the other side of the Alps—if lucky, at ducal courts in Venice and Florence, Milan, and Genova in their native Italy. They spoke in their tongue here to protect their secrets. One over the other, like a chamber orchestra tuning their instruments.

"This was not a good idea."

"It was! I saw him."

"You think you did."

"I thought Giovanna would speak."

"We know nothing about his whereabouts. We shouldn't have come here."

"We had to. Capitano sent us all these expensive clothes."

"He summoned us up here and now sits drunk in his inn!"

"I remember him."

"You were just six at the time, Carlo. You remember nothing, but you think you do."

"I do too."

"Don't be stupid!"

"Francesca is right," said the oldest of the group. "Let's go home."

That same man turned to the official and said, "We have a change of plans. We will come another time."

The official acknowledged that with a short nod. He watched them moving to the end of the large gilded hall, getting smaller and smaller.

Strange people. They come here to disturb and create a case only to change their mind and leave! Such an odd group of strangers although, I have to admit, such interesting, almost wild, expressive faces and also unusually expensive fashions all of them. They do have money. Obviously.

He must point out to the judge that the office is cases short for the autumn, and this case could be it. One must eat and pay taxes—business is business. The judge will return to Vienna, but what about them there? The official hoped he would be able to convince him.

The judge appeared in about an hour. He looked at the paperwork.

"What have we here? Something new to toss?"

He took the visiting card the dubious group left behind on the silver tray.

"Marco Bernini . . . Bernini? Bernini!"

His cheeks changed color. His eyes received a new spark.

"Start a new case folder, Herr Marshalek," he said with absolute certainty, which took the judicial office clerk by surprise. "They will be back."

Magdalena, Frau Ebner, looked out the small window of the kitchen building. There was Thomas following a group of his men carrying some heavy load. Further still, in the linden alley, the Count was holding a large map in his hands, standing under the trees.

Thomas was Count's favorite manager. Magdalena smiled knowingly. Her men—she blushed immediately for it should be only Thomas, but she couldn't help her happy memories. She retied her apron to calm down her thoughts.

Magdalena began counting on her fingers.

The pheasants were shot last Monday so since this is Thursday today, I should start dressing them tomorrow morning, she thought as she counted a few more fingers.

She opened the door to get some fresh air into the kitchen quarters. The gardens, shrubs, grass, and trees all were giving out wet heavy fragrance after the rain. Drops of water gathered above on the door fell down as she opened it, straight behind her neck.

"Ah! Thank goodness it stopped raining."

"Anything from last night's dinner to sink my teeth into?" Thomas asked with hope as he was walking past the door.

Magdalena looked at him, her face brightening up. She stood there making sure he saw the image of her she wanted him to see—clean, warm, inviting. One day she will become Thomas's wife. For now, she has to be patient and clever.

Shoulders of the men walking with Thomas were weighed down with large waxed hemp sacks. Magdalena knew well what was inside. The Countess sent for live fish. Thomas will let them out into the small pond behind the kitchen house. A clear thin stream was redirected there. When time comes, they will be as fresh as when just caught.

"No, Thomas, nothing today, they loved it too much!" she hollered after him. He laughed out loud over his shoulder and went his way.

Magdalena took an empty white pottery milk jug and went to the adjacent pantry room. She put it on the narrow, green painted side table. The door safely closed behind her, she turned towards the deep niche.

She reached above lines of small, gray stoneware jars of last year's marmalades. The one she took out didn't have the waxed cloth fastened by a string, just a small square of washed linen loosely placed over its top.

What the eye can't see, the heart can't grieve over, Magdalena smiled to herself as she was turning the jar to its side.

A piece of last night's dinner cake slid into her fingers. Magdalena closed her eyes and took a bite. She inhaled the warm rich scent of sugar and vanilla. Her neatly combed head dropped back. She exhaled through her turned-up nose; pleasure wrapped around her whole being. The chunk of luscious pastry she so masterfully created yesterday, started melting on her tongue.

Frederik's steps were crushing grass as his riding boots were angrily progressing through the uncut meadow. The grass will need till tomorrow eve to recuperate and raise up before anybody could scythed through it. But he didn't care about such small, unimportant things.

His right hand kept decapitating wild flowers left, right, in the rhythm of his trot.

He had fallen off his horse while his younger brothers were watching. He was beyond furious. He blamed it on the oldest of the nameless group. *Idiot! Saving his puppy from underneath my horse's hoofs!*

"Stupid!"

At first, the small crowd started following him.

"Fred! Wait!"

They didn't want their eldest brother to be upset.

But Frederik, his chin pressed down on the front of his dark blue military jacket, lengthened his steps to alter the distance between him and his brothers, whose names he refused to remember, as quickly as possible.

His mother was watching from her parlor. She saw everything that she herself declined to notice in Frederik's father, her husband, when she first set her mind to marry him—handsome, short-tempered, self-centered, spoilt, unreasonable at times. Her brothers had warned her many times over. They had known him well for years.

They all were a cheerful bunch together at the military academy in Vienna.

At that time, he resided in Vienna. That palace was no more. Such happy memories! He wasn't much interested in her at first. He wasn't keen, it seemed to her, to lose her brothers' friendship. They all went down to Egypt.

Carl-Maria was the only one who returned.

Throughout her grieving, he became her everyday guest—the only one she could stand around. He was tender and attentive to her every wish. Her wealth multiplied many times over. Marie-Adele was her own mistress. The whole new world had opened up for her. He proposed.

Louisa stirred and repositioned the flat, colorful tapestry cushion she was sitting on. Here, hidden behind the broad oakwood column, sheltered from the world by gilded wooden balustrade—this was the perfect reading oasis. The entrance hall was in full view underneath, and she could see without being seen.

Robinson Crusoe, a book " not quite suited for a girl," was resting on her lap. This exciting story was a birthday present from her grandfather, the Count, so not much anybody could say now.

Louisa giggled through her nose—the brief staccato fragments which Frederik loved about her.

Louisa always moved up there from the library after sunlight couldn't reach her through French windows any longer. She opened her book; the scent, mildly pungent, sweet, if peppery, resembled tobacco. Every time grandfather asks her to pass his chamois tobacco pouch, as she opens it, her nose is hit by the heavy smell of dried figs and another intense scent she has no name for yet. She loves when Opa gives her small tasks that nobody else seems to be able to perform as well as she does.

She can't imagine her life without her grandpapa, though she couldn't believe how quickly he stopped talking about her papa after he was killed. Not so Mama. She had been wearing mourning fashions ever since. It has been four years and her looking glass is still adorned by black lace veil.

When she thought about father, Louisa realized that she didn't know him much. Everytime he would come home, it was all about her Mama and Frederik.

Grandfather would always make sure that she stayed as busy as her brother.

There was nothing she couldn't do in his mind. When Frederik got a new horse, Opa made sure she received hers soon after. For his girl, there were no shares, no hand-me-downs. At one time around her last birthday, mother mentioned a perplexing detail. It would seem that grandfather vehemently objected to the name Louisa! Instead of answering Louisa's question she took her down to the library.

A voluminous book in old leather binding revealed the secret. The parchment unfolded. Colorful coat of arms painted all around the edges, this was the von Schönbruck family tree. Mama pointed to the lower space. Grandpapa's name and next to him__Louisa! He never speaks about his late wife. There is no portrait, no miniature.

They say that he made sure nothing was left. No matter how curious, Louisa would never ask.

She was just about to run with Robinson Crusoe to save the man he named Friday from savages (she'd reread this exciting passage at least three times this afternoon) when slight noise from the hallway underneath interrupted her adventures.

She'd almost called down to Frederik, but then she didn't. Something about him didn't feel right. Louisa stopped moving.

Frederik was walking quietly on his bare feet through the long hallway.

Bare feet? Our Frederik?

He quickly glanced around. Louisa froze. She watched his arm stretch above one of the large, tall porcelain containers standing by the wall. She thought she heard a brief muffled sound.

Her curiosity was overpowered by unexplainable fear. It came suddenly, like the shots of misery when she runs barefoot and steps accidentally on sharp stones. Louisa closed her eyes. Her mind slid back behind her ears, and the hum of her blood blocked all other sounds. After a moment, she opened her eyes again and listened, senses on alert.

It was quiet. She carefully peeked through the wooden balusters.

The hallway was empty, not the slightest sign of her brother. Lines of deer trophy mounts stared blindly with their glass eyes straight forward.

She could hear the same conversation still being held in faraway rooms, dogs barking outside in the courtyard, grandfather taking his afternoon nap in the library.

Her confusion was mixed with light dizziness as if she woke up from one of her daydreams.

Mother must be right I am clair—whatever she says I am, Louisa thought.

Since Louisa could not think of any other explanation, she opened the book where her fingers still held it tightly. The last rays of sun touched the wooden wall paneling in the color of ripe rye. Unavoidable sign that she will have to go down to the dining room soon.

She quickly read a few more lines, just in case there was something unexpected. But no, Robinson decided to move Friday to his hut in the fortress…nothing new then.

Louisa stood up, her dress wrinkled; her small, fine-boned foot guided the cushion towards the staircase to drop it down, when the main door burst open.

"Help! Help! It's the young lord! It's Frederik! Help!" the whole house welled up with shouts and screams of horror.

The commotion of people, scared and confused, their voices booming like nothing Louisa had ever heard before, flooded her senses.

Shouts were repeating indoors __ an echo of voices going away, coming back, in and out, back again; chaos of men running, explaining, deciding what to do; their voices louder, multiplying as more people were pulled into this mayhem.

Louisa was glued to her spot, observing in silent shock the sudden burst of panic underneath. Then there was grandfather running out of the library.

He was there just in time to catch Frederik in his arms.

"God! My boy, you are covered in blood? Are you hurt?" his voice boomed through the lodge. "Help me here someone! Now! I need help!"

He cradled his grandson in his arms, his tone changed to softness unusual for such a strongly built tall man.

"Fred," he whispered with tenderness, "what's happened? Fred, dear boy, tell your grandpa. Are you injured?"

Frederik was in shock. His body was shivering as he tried to talk.

"I l-lost her. I c-couldn't f-find h-her. I-I was look-king . . . w-whistling. I could-dn't s-save her . . . and th-then . . . there there!"

He was pointing out, shouting other words, incomprehensible at first.

Finally they all understood. Count kept holding his grandson's shaking body, now wrapped by some good hand in a large blue woolen scarf.

Count was giving orders to his men in rapid sequence as if he were back on the battlefield. Everyone took tools, weapons—

anything they were able to find. Armed, they rushed out the door towards the forest. Fredrik, who insisted on showing them the way, was more carried by the strong arms of his grandfather than walking, pointing in front of them, out into the woods.

They ran across the park then up the short slope where the forest started.

"There! There!" Frederik was breathless, exhausted by his sobs.

In a puddle of blood lay his sweet bitch Duchess. Her eyes without life, her body covered with numerous stabbing wounds. Fredrik pushed out from his grandfather's arms and dropped on her, crying.

Smudged by her blood all over again, he kept hugging her dead body.

"My Duchess, my darling, forgive me! Please, please . . . forgive me!"

"You couldn't have protected her. It was a madman who'd done this!" Count tried to reason with his grandson, whose tears were mixing with blood on his face, removing him from the scene.

It took Leopold all his strength to make the grieving boy leave his dead dog's side. Frederik's cries seemed to have no end; he was in tears all night. His temperature rose to dangerous heights.

The Countess's doctor bled him several times but didn't see what more could be done. They waited. Countess von Schönbruck sat down on the narrow bed of her eldest son. She took Frederik's hand in hers. Deep in thoughts, not in prayers anymore, she found herself caressing his forehead.

This was the first time in years she allowed herself to touch her own child in this intimate way. She wept quietly for years after all the little bodies she delivered to the world, little lives who perished in front of her helpless eyes. She mourned all of her motherly love, lost forever.

Luckily, before noon, Fredrik's temperature had dropped, and he fell asleep.

Mother kissed his cheeks, pulled the light curtains on his bed halfway open, and left him alone. Nanny put the bowl with vinegar-induced water on the small table. Then she sat down in a chair by Frederik's bed and began to knit.

The Countess tried not to make a sound as she was coming down the wooden staircase. Through the door left ajar, she saw her father-in-law, still in his low armchair in the library. She didn't want to wake him up; he was at her side all night long.

But Leopold Count von Schönbruck didn't sleep. He was far from resting; he couldn't rid his mind of his growing suspicions, of his paralyzing fear.

Is this revenge? A first hint of what could happen next? A small message? From whom? Count's mind produced sweet faces of his beloved grandchildren. He shivered. *No no. I have to hold tight to reason. There is no way someone could have recognized me! After decades? No . . . Or could they?*

He didn't want to admit fear—the word he despised. But it was making way through his brain, logging to his veins, running through his body. He was powerless against such an invasion. His secret maneuver was useless here.

Maybe it's time to go away after all, to visit Weimar again. To stay away for a year or more.

Count opened his eyes. That seemed like the best idea. He sat up sharply.

"Do you wish something, my lord?" His old Johann stood up from his chair by the door.

Leopold shook his head no. Then he noticed how tired his old servant looked. "Go to bed, Johann, I'll be fine."

Not even waiting for Johann to leave, Count walked to his study and sat down to write to his friend Goethe in Weimar.

A soft knock on her forehead woke Louisa up unpleasantly early, as usual.

In summertime, children were not allowed to miss morning dew.

After running in cold, wet grass in the garden—for good health—they competed in running up to the house to change for breakfast. The fastest one would have the first choice of one of Magdalena's sweet breakfast buns.

Louisa stayed behind. She looked around in all directions just as her brother had done the day before. Certain that she was not being watched, she pulled up on her tiptoes and peeked into the tall vase. Louisa exhaled, disappointed. The vase was empty.

Really? she seethed, her fragile shoulders dropping lower than usual. *Just another vivid daydream?*

A door opened somewhere, and Louisa heard her name being called with a slight tint of impatience.

She glanced at her reflection in the nearby glass door pane, running her slim fingers through her short "Titus." "Better!" she smiled and only then ran upstairs towards the voice.

Louisa took the stairs to the upper floor two at once. Breathlessly she stopped in front of the nanny.

"I'm here, Mademoiselle!"

Nanny gave Louisa an inspecting glance, picking the front of Louisa's morning dress in pinch.

"Now, really, little Countess? How did this happen?" She shook her aging head, white low chignon bounced together with the pristine laces of her bonnet.

Louisa looked down, and her mind went blank. Among the flowers of the busy chintz print were spots of dark red. Louisa knew exactly what they were—she realized right away where she got them and turned pale.

"You shouldn't be painting without wearing your frock! How many times do I . . ."

But Louisa couldn't hear the rest. She turned with uncharacteristic rudeness and, without any explanation, ran outside.

Someone was sitting on the edge of his bed who was not his nanny.

I am having a nightmare, Frederik thought, coughing.

"Good morning, my little boy," said the woman simply, smiling and stretching her arm to caress his hair. "You look much better this morning."

Frederik's silence didn't make her uncomfortable.

"You should have some broth now," Maria-Antonia, Countess von Schönbruck, his mother, said, standing up. She reached for a small, white, gilded porcelain cup.

She insisted on waiting on her son that morning. She ladled some hot broth in it and picked up the silver spoon. She placed a towel under his chin.

"Here, my darling, it will make you stronger."

Frederik had no energy to turn his head away quickly enough. Her long cold fingers full of amethyst rings reached towards his head.

Couldn't she wear something else? Father must have given her troves of jewels!

She flattened the front of his hair. Frederik was furious. His lips pressed together as he was looking away.

His mother sat down and lifted the bowl under his chin. She tried the broth herself first. Its temperature was just fine. The taste was rich as only Magdalena knew how to prepare such delicacy.

The Countess carried the full spoon towards Frederik's dry lips and said, "Here, my baby, have some. It's nice and warm."

He felt hungry but didn't want to give her any satisfaction. He was too weak to hit the hand. To make a scene. To throw a tantrum. He longed for the sound of fine family china breaking to pieces on the parquets. His anger took away the rest of his energy.

If only I were not so exhausted!

The silver spoon clicked on Frederik's tightly locked front teeth. He hated the feeling and opened his mouth.

Summer was rolling lazily in this valley under the majestic Alps. Louisa wrote some short little poems early in the morning. She would leave them around the park. "For Mother Nature!" she explained to the nannies.

She overheard them saying "Naive." Since she was not certain what it meant exactly, she didn't mind. She'll ask Opa sometime today. Louisa's frock was washed and back in her wardrobe. That curious memory lingered in her mind. She was tempted to ask Fred about it once he's well again.

Now she was in the wilderness of the English park, standing up to her knees in the cold stream. She was trying to show her young brothers how to catch a trout with a spear, the way Robinson Crusoe would have done.

Two young boys, helping with turning hay in the meadow, came to drink from the stream. They rolled up their brown hemp pants and climbed down to the water. A little further up the stream from the noble children they watched them from a safe distance. After a moment, the older of the two got courage and walked closer.

"Are you trying to catch trout?"

Louisa took several steps towards the boy.

"Yes, but no such luck."

"We could show you."

Louisa looked at her brothers. They all were excited at the prospect, so she nodded, her short hair bouncing up and down.

"All right then, you may show us!"

When they came close, she stretched her arm to hand them her spear.

"Here."

"What do you have that pole for?"

"It's a spear, of course!"

"A spear?"

"What's wrong with the spear? Robinson inadvertently—"

"What?"

"Oh, never mind. Show us then! How do you want to catch fish without a tool?"

"You must be quiet, first of all. They won't come here now. You disturbed them for the day. We must walk up the stream."

Louisa enthusiastically decided for all at once.

"Yes, let's!"

"And you all must stay quiet. Fish do listen, you know?"

The kids giggled.

"Fish can't hear!"

"Yes they can!"

"They can? They can hear?" The little blond and dark-brown pates shook in disbelief, their mouths opened.

"They are listening just like you or me even right now" revealed the village boy.

The von Schönbruck children were in awe. Now they walked quietly behind those two slightly frightening village boys. They kept hush until one of the strange boys turned his palm against the little crowd signaling "Stop!"

With eyes wide open, children watched him make slow-motion steps in cold water. The stream enclosed briskly his bare legs.

They all stood in silence, their anticipation stretched like the bow Louisa made for them yesterday.

Then the boy suddenly shot his arms into the cold stream and then again and again! Three trout were wiggling in the grass.

Instead of applause, Louisa started shouting "You must kill them! They suffer! They can't breathe!"

"They can't breathe!" echoed her young siblings one over the others.

Their new acquaintances hopped out from the stream, dripping wet, shouting back, "Stop! You're screaming! You stupid! Stupid!"

"Kill them, kill them, please quickly!" Louisa was beside herself.

"Quickly, quickly!" Her small brothers were bouncing around.

The village boys did that skillfully with one strong poke through the spine by fish tails, then turned towards the noble kids.

"They are all gone for today! You can go home now."

They cut three long sticks from a basket willow tree. The stump-like short, thick, dark brown trunks kept holding the creak in its waterbed by roots. The bright green sticks were pushed longways through the trout.

"Who is going to carry them back home?" asked the older boy and created another mayhem.

Both young strangers started laughing and turned to go away.

Louisa had to decide quickly. "Carl and Zvonimir and you, Tommi, halfway to the big pine tree, then you, Aloys to the . . ."

She explained her plan; it was fair. They all agreed about their divided duties.

There was no thank-you to the fishermen, but they all waved enthusiastically after them; the village boys were already back on the sun-flooded meadow; with the wooden rakes in hand, they kept turning the grass their fathers cut early in the morning. Strong, sweet scent reached Louisa's nose. Freshly cut grass, drying hay, scent of pages when she opened a book—that was her very own summer.

Then she thought of Frederik and poor tragic Duchesse, such a sweet. Unsettling questions made her almost cry like ice-cold snow balls which hurt when Frederik pushes them into her neckline in winter. She started rushing towards home. Her little brothers could hardly keep up.

Frederik couldn't recall the last time his mother came and sat down by his bed or even visited his bedroom. Maybe she was never here, he thought. He made no effort to remember. He was exhausted.

It was his father who was there all the time. His father had come very often. Yes! He's sure of it! His own Papa. Only for him, only for *his* Frederik!

He was always there, for real, only for him. He would teach him and explain things to him. He would show him which tools were for what and how to make the watermill from broken branches they found during their walk. He showed him how to cut them, carve the propellers, and construct them into a small water wheel which they would place in the narrow stream in the park later. *Wait, what is Thomas doing in this memory?*

Oh yes, he must have brought the branches and cut them into sticks and peel them and cut small, short propellers out of them, and then_ it was all too confusing now! Frederik stirred. Mother sat up straight watching her boy with alarmed eyes. She relaxed as he seemed to be just dreaming again.

Frederik wanted to remember his father's warm body behind him on his horse forever. Happy moment when someone's arms would lift Frederik, the little boy, laughing of joy, up to his father's saddle. And off they went! Trotting first.

"Can you feel the rhythm, Fred? She is going on the right leg. Now wait! We'll start galloping and then hop! Let's change her to the left leg and then back!"

Once they were out of sight, his father would hit a horse's rump, and they charged forward the speed of wind! Oh, the excitement!

Papa . . . He was always with me. But Mother? That strangely remote thin person? She always seemed to be somehow ill. Her dress would always be bulging in the front. When he would ask, she would say that there's a new baby. *Under her dress? Silly!*

He asked his nanny; she would giggle, making no attempt to explain. But then there was no baby in the end.

Mother is lying! Frederik was sure.

Then one day, out of the blue, a little baby was unexpectedly there. *She wasn't lying! At least this once.*

They named her Louisa, after the Prussian queen, whom her mother had idolized.

Louisa was now his sister and the youngest. She was christened quickly in her mother's bedchamber that very day. Her full name was noted as Louisa Antonia Gudrun Maria Countess von Schönbruck. They didn't expect her to live long.

But she proved stronger than her petite, fragile frame had suggested.

They made for her little cloth bundles filled with crushed spinach, honey, and herbs to suck on; they laid an oval basket with soft wool skeins and cotton scarves; they placed the basket in the gray stoneware baking dish. Then they put the baby in, and off to the deep, warm niche behind the always-lit tile stove.

It had been standing high in its green, glossy beauty in the corner for at least a century. Pots with chicory coffee were kept there; shoes were put there to dry in winter.

Frederik called the little baby girl secretly "Our Baked Louisa." He said it only once out loud when he thought nobody was around. It was quite a smack that flew behind his ear; his grandfather, the Count, was standing round the corner.

Frederik remembered the day he was finally allowed to see his new little baby sister. She was standing by her nanny dressed in red. Her dress was long and her baby pantaloons wide. A baby-bumper safely around her head, she was holding her ear for support. Then suddenly she took a few steps and sat down on the floor.

He loved how she smiled at him. Anything he would do amused her. He submitted to a silly clown position gladly, to everyone's amazement. It was easy for him; unknowingly, tiny Louisa already spoiled him by laughing and giggling at his crazy movements and daft faces.

This new feeling was completely unexpected for him. She had become his new, true friend. He fell in love with her. She was no threat to his life—she was a girl!

Mother's cool fingers caressed Frederik some more. She placed the half-empty bowl of broth—now cold—back on the side table. There was no strength in Frederik to speak, to say, "I don't want you here!" To scream at her,

"I want my Papa! I want him back, and you I wish gone forever! All of you!" He closed his eyes and fell back to sleep.

Poor Duchess was already buried in the park when Frederik was allowed to go out. He put wildflowers on her grave. He would do it the next day, then the next one.

Then he returned to his games and riding. He would never mention the unlucky dog again.

Frau Ebner gave up looking for the misplaced knife, and she reached for a different one. She exclaimed out loud in surprise. Her favorite butcher's knife was at the exact spot where she always found it. Was it weeks now?

She shook her head. "My knife!"

Then her surprise turned into embarrassment which prompted a cute chuckle. "What a mystery."

"Mystery? Ha! it's your old age!" countered Thomas who just brought some pine cones for her stove.

She shushed him away with laughter, hitting him playfully with her fresh, clean apron which she just unfolded.

She shouted amidst giggles, "Out you go!"

The apron had a small bouquet of edelweiss embroidered on its front. Magdalena did it herself. She stepped back to the vast table and started chopping carrots; her favorite knife felt duller than she remembered. She took the sharpening steel out of the drawer and gave it a few quick up-and-down motions.

"You are like a swordsman, woman!" Thomas was back with more firewood.

Magdalena laughed, "Hardly, but I can slap your deerskins flat with it just fine!"

She turned the large knife to its side. He tossed the armful of precisely chopped beechwood in the niche by the stove and turned to face her.

"Help! An armed woman!"

His hands were shaking up in the air, pretending to be running away and bumped into the young boy who came after him, sending his basket full of small pine cones flying across the kitchen.

The boy froze, waiting for a shower of nasty swear words, but instead, the two old people in front of him kept giggling. They knelt down side by side to help the poor frightened boy to pick up small fragrant cones brought in for a quick flame.

"You, woman!" whispered Thomas close to Magdalena's face, raising his voice after. "You know nothing about how much I fancy you. Had you not that knife in your hand, I would have . . ."

"You would have what, Thomas?" giggled Clara, the always eavesdropping redhead who came back with a large jug full of water.

"Clara, put the jug on the table and take a knife for dandelion leaves!"

Magdalena knew Thomas's answer too well. There was not enough in his pocket—yet—to make living for both them and their potential family. They had to leave it at that, for now.

They were not exactly young anymore—she in her late thirties, Thomas pushing forty.

Magdalena stood up and shook her apron clean. She walked up to Thomas, placed her strong-boned small palm, full of burns and scratches, on his ruddy cheek.

"Thank you, Thomas."

She hoped he would kiss her hand, but with the presence of extra pairs of eyes, he instead mumbled

"No problem" and walked out around Clara.

Magdalena looked at the redhead and said, "What do you know about life?"

Clara was standing there, backlit, a glowing red line around her hair like a halo.

"And what happened to the leaves?" Frau Ebner reminded her.

Clara ran out through the back door to the potage garden right away.

Magdalena made a short mental note to herself, *Sharpen the butcher's knife!*

"Thank you, Grandfather!" called the Count after his little twin grandsons.

Rhythmical slapping of their feet on large slate tiles in the corridor revealed that they were already too far for another "good manners" lesson of his.

A gentle shuffle of soft summer slippers turned Count von Schönbruck's head. It was his eldest granddaughter. She just peeked into the library and waved at him. Before he could call any greetings, she was outside, running with her much younger siblings. He heard nannies calling with concerns about the speed of that lively sibling steeplechase. He must talk to her soon about his leaving.

He never wanted to mark one of his grandchildren as his favorite; Louisa, however, not only had the most pleasant appearance, she was also bright, always interested in everything he'd told her.

If he'd mentioned a book, he would find her reading it, even at times when she couldn't possibly understand a word of it yet.

Her love for words became his fascination with her. "Come, read with Grandpapa!" he would say loudly in the direction where she was playing. He knew that it would take only a second; and his little girl would dust her hands, put her doll under her arm, and rush up to him.

She grew up into a lovely girl, twelve years old just like that.

His happiness could be destroyed with one word. That must not happen. He must go away.

He will miss her. Them all. It's for the best. His mind was made up. He was to leave this coming Monday.

The moment Leopold opened his book it was like magic. His mind was clear, and he calmed down as he was invited to the new story. As on every other occasion, it unrevealed itself page after page, posing questions, meandering to highs and lows of human existence. Count read until he realized that he no longer heard his voice. He read silently for the first time in his life, and it felt right and very intimate—a feeling he had been always looking for but hadn't realized how easy to get.

He relaxed, and everything—the whole world out there—ceased to exist.

Thoughts which he never would have been able to formulate himself—unlocked mechanisms of his brain which he'd never have guessed lived within him.

He stepped freely to the flow of storytelling as if it were a river taking his doubts and fears away.

The little group of strangers in fine clothes were back. Herr Marshalek—his pince-nez firmly clutching his bulbous nose—smiled at them. He had his instructions.

"Which one of you is Carlo?"

The small crowd reacted as if the named young man, their cousin, had an infectious disease.

"He is!"

Carlo suddenly stood there as an abandoned prop mid stage.

"I am . . ."

For over a decade, there was no need to revisit those horrid days.

He was just a boy of about six who loved sweets. His big cousins Gabriel and Giovanna used to bring him handfuls when they needed his help. If he kept his mouth shut, he'd get more of Turkish honey.

A Turk in a red fez with black tassel, all dressed in purple with white sheet to cover his front, stood by a block of his specialty, the confection which stood in a puddle of honey like a white-and-gold island. Each time he lifted his hatchet, the puff of wasps shot above him. Carlo adored the whole spectacle and still feels the honey on his tongue.

"Herr Judge is expecting you." Herr Marshalek pointed at the door behind him, partly obscured by a heavy velvet curtain with golden tassels.

Carlo feared his uncle Marco, Giovanna's father. He wasn't certain how bad it could turn for him. Although just a little boy then, Marco, his uncle, suspected that he knew more than he told him.

"His Honor is waiting," Herr Marshalek said, pushing the young man.

Carlo woke up; as the servant opened the tall gilded door, he walked hesitantly in.

Several minutes to their conversation, there was nothing the judge could use.

"Think about all that, and you'll tell me more the next time."

Carlo knew that this man didn't buy his "I was too little to remember" ruse.

He was right. Carlo was lying. He walked out of the office, and all eyes were at him.

He shrugged his shoulders, said "I know nothing," and then he crossed to the far window and leaned against its frame.

Someone else was called in. Carlo looked out the window. The street was narrow; he could watch someone else's life at the small town palace across. They were having hot chocolate and some pastries. Carlo could see the sugar-dusted buns.

He would always have a pocketful of Turkish honey slivers wrapped tightly in parchment that Gab would bribe him with. He remembered vividly watching from top of the ladder as Giovanna sneaked out of the yard. Carlo was up there in the opening of the barn front, sitting on hay. Kittens were up there with their mother. He and other kids were allowed by the innkeeper's wife to climb up and play with them.

He didn't hesitate. He would slide down from the light wooden ladder and run to tell Gabriel.

It wasn't hard to find him. He was trying on a new costume that Carlo's mother fitted for him. It was full of glistening silver embellishments.

As the sun was going down, the long, thin, silver painted hangings would reflect the last glints of light on his sleeves. Carlo remembered how amazing they looked; when Gab moved, they looked positively like blades.

Louisa stopped writing.

How should I put this? she thought for a moment.

Then she hung up the pencil back on her silver chatelaine. She was at a loss and crumpled the sheet of paper.

If you want to clear your thoughts, write them down, says Grandpapa.

"It's easy to say, Opa." She made a funny grimace towards the ceiling.

If her Grandpa were there, they could have giggled together. But not now; he was probably packing his books.

Her thoughts kept going; however, even now, they became too quick for her to be able to write them down. She thought for a moment. As always, it suddenly came to her. She knew exactly what to do. Her mind was pushy, not willing to stop. Louisa had to pick up speed.

Mother says I am sometimes clear—no, it is clair_. . . Louisa wasn't sure how to spell it now.

Her memory kept rushing forward regardless. "Oh, nevermind!" Louisa took another sheet of paper.

My chintz dress got dirty there, smudged by something brown.

Here she decided not to acknowledge what she truly thought for now. It was very confusing and scary.

Anyway, Fred was heartbroken. Oh he was so devastated!

Her thoughts paused, and she plunged back into her early memories.

It was just like when I found my little doll, Mieschen. She was all broken, I thought he would surely get ill with how much he cried for my little doll. Such a soft heart, our Fred. Oh how he cried for his Duchess! It was heartbreaking, yes. It was just like when he cried for my little doll, when she got so, so horribly shredded and stabbed through and through.

Louisa's thoughts stopped there as abruptly as if she pulled reins of her horse; she was looking straight ahead into empty space. Still without any breath coming out of her childlike full lips, she stood up.

There was her book, *Robinson Crusoe*, her friend. Her eyes filled up with a reassuring smile, and only then, she exhaled. Slowly, with care, such as when she would pick up an injured kestrel in the woods, she lifted up her favorite book—her new closest friend—from the floor.

She held it against her girly flat chest, enclosed in a tight embrace; her eyes were shut again, her lips were moving. In one moment, it sounded a bit as if she said "Forgive me" but one couldn't be sure—that's how low, strictly confidential she'd kept her voice that afternoon.

"What now?"

Giovanna turned, already half undressed. But all happened so swiftly, she didn't have time to step behind her Japanese screen. The stagehand brought in a message right away as it said URGENT. Giovanna's maid took it from him and pushed him out of the dressing room into the sparsely lit corridor.

"It came through a messenger!" he hardly had time to tell her.

Giovanna recognized the seal and turned pale.

When she opened the letter, it was a brief note which said in her father's clumsy handwriting,

"You will regret it!"

Giovanna's color returned to her cheeks and turned crimson. She was angry.

That man thinks that he could manipulate my life again? No! No, I will not do anything.

Whatever might happen next she was right not to give any details in Innsbruck. She will not testify; she will not ruin someone's life. Giovanna tossed the note, but its tone stayed with her.

She poured herself some water from the simple jug on the white painted side table, then called her maid to undress her.

Just in her white silk bustier and short pantaloons, she sat down in front of the looking glass. Two candles from each side were not enough, but she knew her face well. She heard noises from the corridor as the first chorus girls started arriving with their gentlemen friends. She heard dressers complaining about that nightly torn sleeve; and someone's answer "He holds me too tight!" and laughter and giggle. *What do they know about life?*

She reached for her wooden *schminken kiste*, the makeup box, which used to be her mother's.

Time to choose the right rouge for her lips to match her opening-scene red dress. She took the small porcelain jar and put it closer to her mirror. Next, she used the rabbit's paw to carefully tap powder over her white makeup.

She scooped some rouge on her middle finger tip and dabbed her cheeks.

Her eyebrows and eye contours were next. She opened a small jar where she stored her very own paint for eyelashes. She'd mixed it herself, the way women of her family have been doing for centuries—ashes mixed with juices of elderberries and a little drop of oil. Only she knew the formula. There was no counting but a little song; the beginning of each stanza was the time for another ingredient. Its magic had cast spells over her audiences, time and time again. Superstitious, she'd have never admitted that perhaps, her large expressive eyes had the magic within them.

A loud knock on the door announced one of her admirers.

"Desiree?"

"Judge!"

Giovanna smiled and, without care for putting on her kimono, called, "Come on in, darling!"

She was glad that she didn't apply rouge on her lips yet.

The young kitchen help, the gossip-loving redhead, Clara, was walking down the sand path to the icebox. With every careful step she was recounting all she had done to this point since early morning.

She was easily distracted; she must make sure all was done, not like the other day.

So_all apples were turned and inspected and carefully laid back into shallow straw-packed baskets, then carried back to the shelves in the fruit cellar. Carrots were inspected in their sand lodging and potatoes turned and selected in the vegetable chamber. Eggs counted and numbered. Icebox now. The last thing she had to do today. She never mind the walk.

She liked it there. She looked around. The nearest people were way back. Men were leading horses to water them down in the river. She unhooked her tight bustier and sat down. A moment there was worth any yelling or cursing if anybody saw her and told Magdalena.

Clara's hair was neatly combed back; she wouldn't have it otherwise. Her copper-colored braids were tightly pinned into a low bun in the back of her head. The nuns taught them well in the orphanage. She was called the Devil's child_ redhead and all. She wondered sometimes who her mother was. Looking for redheads in markets. Fantasizing about a nice family. It was all to no avail. She shook her head. *Guard your thoughts!* Frau Ebner says.

Clara's crisp white linen cap was fixed with two wide ribbons—no one could tell that they were made from the same old bed sheets as the cap.

She tied them under her round chin. Her rosy cheeks were pushed forward, slightly flushed from the quick walking she did to give herself extra time here. Her complexion seemed translucent.

She looked like a Meissen porcelain doll. But she didn't know it. She'd never stepped into the house where the fine Maissen porcelain was on display.

She was a very mature seventeen-year-old. Men turned their heads when she came to dance on Saturday nights.

Icebox! There it was. Placed by the trout stream, its steep roof covered in slate, this was the oldest surviving construction on the estate. It served as an icebox for centuries. It was built against a short, rocky slope.

The Secret Maneuver

The whitewashed building stood in the cool part of the lower park. Inside, an eternal water spring kept gushing from the middle of a massive sand rock. The basin carved softly in the large mineral kept overflowing. Its perpetual stream never tired of adding another layer to the ring of colorful sediments, before vanishing back to the underground.

This water was much tastier than the one from the old well in the courtyard. Some drank from the river too; but it was mostly brought up for cooking, washing dishes, and for bathing on Fridays.

Clara filled large crates with spring water earlier that morning there. Thomas helped her carry them up in the house. She neither minded his wandering hands nor his brief kisses. She knows that he loves Magdalena.

Clara would have never dreamed of coming between them. *Although,* she thought, *Thomas is quite the man.*

Ice blocks were packed up high, all around the walls. Stoneware pots and urns of all sizes and shapes—their lids sealed airtight with beeswax—were standing close to the ice. Those were smoked meat pâtés, pickled venison gizzards, and such.

It was cold like on a January day down there. Such a nice change from the heat of the open fire and smoke of the black kitchen. Clara put the oil lamp on the ground and pulled her large woolen scarf tightly around her body. She walked forward then stopped and listened. She thought she heard steps behind her, but the sound stopped when she stopped. She's not the one made for fear. She turned.

"May I help you, my lord?"

Beam of her lantern wasn't strong enough, but she saw him.

"Count Frederik?"

The young Count was standing there, just a few yards behind her, looking straight at her. He didn't answer. He didn't stop looking at her either.

Around them was silence, cut in short segments by percussion of dripping ice melting away into drains carved in the rock floor.

"I'm here to get some ice for the sweet treat," Clara broke the awkward stillness; she didn't mind continuing her soliloquy. "For after dinner . . . you know."

She held forward a small thick-wall stoneware pot she was carrying. Her scarf slipped to one side, her full bodice offered the silhouette of her breasts. She didn't hurry to fix it.

Frederik didn't move. Clara noticed his face.

Eyes set far apart, handsome, in a wild, somewhat strange, dangerous way.

She had never seen him like that until now.

He's become quite a strong young man already.

She pushed into a new territory when she said, "You like the red currant one and the raspberry sherbet too, I hear."

She looked him straight in the eyes. Her lips felt suddenly dry, and she slowly licked her top lip, left to right. Frederik's eyes were fixed on her breasts. Clara was more naive than she knew. She sailed through her teens with all the luck imaginable. Now her excitable imagination ran wild.

Maybe he likes me. Oh, I hope he does. Maybe he'll come closer and kiss me.

She lifted her left arm to show him the small hatchet she came armed with down here.

"I always chop it with this little hatchet," she told the young Count. "Our Thomas sharpened it for me just now in the kitchen."

She hoped to break his silence, to give him reason to talk to her, to encourage him. She really liked him.

"And then Frau Ebner would—"

Frederik turned and ran away.

Clara shook her head, "Crazy! Poor boy. Almost a man of fifteen!"

She was glad those growing-up days were behind her now.

She walked across the room, fixed the large pin on her breasts, and pulled the woolen scarf closer to her chest. As she started chipping away the large block of ice, a little song, in three, came to her mind. She started singing it and chopping in the rhythm.

"Is o-ur love strong enough, that no hatchet will break its tuft . . ."

She swayed her hips, her skirts dancing in the rhythm of her favorite ländler. She kept singing and chopping, supplying words which she'd forgotten with cheerful, fearless "la-la-las."

Clara couldn't wait for Saturday evening to dance down in the village. Her eyes turned into narrow crescents in a spontaneous smile; her full lips pressed on all her small white teeth.

She didn't give Frederik one more thought.

"Do we have . . . fomething . . . fome . . . glue, Magda?"

The kind Frau Ebner looked down, her eyebrows changing position to a higher ground.

"It's Frau Ebner, and what did you break this time, my little angel?"

She put the list of provisions that the Count was requesting for his trip on the oak desk. Large mug with some leftover chicory coffee was put to work as a paperweight. Magdalena pushed back the simple pinewood chair with the back of her legs and stood up.

Little Sophie, the youngest of the von Schönbruck siblings, was hopping from one of her almost-four-year-old feet to the other, unable to stand still. When she stopped, she started immediately bouncing up and down in the anticipation of problems.

Her head full of dark curls kept making short sways forward and back with her every word as she chanted, "I did not!"

Then she stepped closer to Magdalena. Her upper body in a light gauze dress tilted forward, her head helping her to syncopate her words.

"I have it fouw fome-one," she said quickly with a slight hint of impatience.

"Oh, that's a secret then, isn't it?" Magdalena whispered dramatically, her eyes opening wide, a tender smile within her question, winking at the little messenger.

The little shoulders in a short, white summer dress went up and down—not a word.

Magdalena—Frau Ebner—turned and her serious index finger said it with her "Wait here."

Then she walked outside and across the small neatly swept courtyard.

She unlocked the heavy door and walked inside the adjacent pantry. Past the last shelf on the left was a niche carved in the granite wall block. She kept special tinctures and other stuff which needed more cold in there. That's where she kept the glue.

"Now, both hands." The little palms were arranged into a well where she placed the small, gray earthen jar. With the highly serious 'Don't break it' executed in a low voice she looked the little girl straight in her hazel eyes.

The cute lisp came again. Little Sophie was whispering slowly, giving utmost importance to every word,

"I muft not tell a-ny-bo-dy."

She took a few careful hesitant steps. Then she stopped and took pity on her kind helper,"It if a feekwit."

Her curls bounced up and down in an accord before she walked away, mincing her steps in fear of dropping her treasure.

Magdalena's smile rearranged all her wrinkles into an upward set of little fans. She wondered whose shoes were going to be stuck to the floor this time. It made her chuckle out loud. She would have never told on any of the little crowd and had been adored for that.

Except for Fredrik, of course. Poor boy. He is another story. Good boy but . . .

"He's odd," she heard herself say out loud.

"Who's odd?" said the deep voice behind her.

Magdalena turned and smacked Thomas's shoulder.

"Oh, Thomas! You startled me."

She was quickly brushing his shirt with intimate playfulness at the spot where her palm hit.

"I meant Frederik," Frau Ebner said.

"What about him?"

Thomas pointed to the helper where to place the two heavy pails full of potatoes on the floor and sent the young boy away. Then he leaned over the working table. Magdalena handed him a thick slice of bread.

"Goose fat?" she asked.

"Oh, yes," Thomas chortled hopefully.

She smeared the slice and seduced him even further, "Onion?"

"Yes, please."

Thomas loved everything about Magdalena but would have to admit that her cooking was on top.

"I don't know, Thomas. I think to be the only child, the heir, everything centered around you for years then overnight—poof! All gone. Surrounded by unexpected siblings, and then the worst, his father killed."

"Well. . .He wasn't here much anyways," Thomas put the last chunk of bread in his mouth and stretched his back. "Aaah!"

Then he leaned back down on the table across from Magdalena. He finished chewing and placed his closely shaved face on the Y of his hands.

"He was a true soldier, you know, and a hussar at that. Oh did he love being a hussar."

Magdalena handed him a wet cloth. "Poor Countess."

Thomas wiped his mouth with his hardened palms. "The boy will be fine."

He took the blue jug with water from her hand and replaced it with the cloth.

"Look at me! I am fine, and if I told you . . ." He took a sip and put the jug back in her hands.

"Don't!" she laughed, pushing him off the table. "We have no time for that! That's if we are going to that Saturday dance. We are going, right?"

He stood up straight, nodded yes, and quickly kissed her nape as she already turned away.

"Saturday! That's for certain, old girl," Thomas laughed, walking out to the rest of this hot day.

The letter from her father, addressed simply "To Desiree," was delivered by a messenger, right before her performance. She could have tossed it. But her curiosity!

He was writing with utmost authority—coldly, without any hint of their relation. He spoke to the judges and that Giovanna should expect a letter from the Highest Imperial Court, for she will be summoned up to come and testify in a murder trial where she was to be the crown witness and as such also the prime suspect!

He already painted the scandal it would cause in vivid, malicious colors, contoured by suggested blackmail.

She sat down, breathless. She heard her father's voice—his irony, his drunken laughter.

Giovanna's temples were pounding; her throat turned dry.

"Five minutes!" the call came, relentless and nonnegotiable.

She was all dressed up for Juliet.

"Get ready, Madame," her dresser said as she walked in, looking at Desiree with concern. "Did you fall ill?"

"Yes, I think I am unwell."

A burst of noise from the audience reached them here.

"You must go there. Now."

"I can't! I can't…" Desiree's voice died out as she looked at her maid.

Then the stage manager called again, now in the doorway, "Juliet! Come!"

Desiree was briskly ushered forward. Someone's hands tapped her smudged face and another hand pushed her on the stage.

She heard herself laugh, she felt herself dancing, and she heard her voice bright with love, talking from the balcony, shouting in desperation and crying and dying.

Then the performance was over. She didn't recall walking away from the sound of applause; she had no idea how she got back into her dressing room adorned by bouquets after bouquets.

Now she was sitting in front of her mirror. Her costume was drenched. Long minutes had passed, and her maid placed the dish with pork fat in front of her, pressed folded hemp cloth in her hand.

"Madame, wipe your face please. It's getting late."

The door opened, and her fans were pushing in—men, admirers, lovers, and some theatre-loving wealthy ladies. She was still in her costume when her world spun around, and all went blank.

"Going for berries?" Clara, the small redhead—curious as usual—called after Louisa and Frederik.

Hand in hand, clutching white clay jugs, they were jogging past her.

Her hands were busy with wooden pegs, fixing wet sheets to hemp lines running from a laundry pole to another—eight total on the meadow behind the house.

She received no answer.

Youngsters! Noble, eh? Don't even bother answering! They'll never find anything. Look at them holding hands like two babies! she thought, envious. *Just you wait, I'll show you on Saturday how to dance!*

"Clara! What are you doing?" called Frau Ebner from the kitchen doorway.

"Hanging kitchen laundry. It's Thursday."

"Well, leave it there and come home soon. Look at the clouds."

Clara looked up and crossed herself. The skies were darkening, although the sun was still shining, pinching her freckled skin.

Gray clouds, like dirty foam on top of water after she washed the kitchen floor, were rushing over the forests. Mountains on the horizon were already obscured, and Clara could smell water in the air.

She grabbed the small basket with the rest of laundry pegs, tossed it on top of the wet laundry, and lifted the heavy load. The wicker basket was making dangerous noises, but she took it all at once. She had to use all her strength to walk briskly towards the house. When she entered, the first raindrops fell heavily on the meadow.

She didn't care to tell anybody about the two pickers heading to the forest.

Serves them well, she thought.

A thunderbolt cut the sky in half; a deafening crack scared all—humans and animals. Clara lit the Saint Medard candle.

Giovanna was resting on the chaise longue before her evening performance. Her room was filled with flowers. She went back on the stage the next day after falling ill. She will not allow that silly young understudy to play her parts!

She wished father had reconsidered. But Gabriel was the talent he always hoped his own sons would show. He pictured himself as his wealthy impresario! Such a dark business, it was.

Her thoughts were not ready to give her any rest today. Giovanna closed her eyes.

Gab was her cousin—her mother's late brother's boy. His mother died of fever when he was a little child. They grew up together, acted in plays together. They slept in one bed. Giovanna's smile turned into a tender glow.

They put them next to each other as kids. When lights were out, they would hear adults in the bed next to them. They got used to falling asleep to lovemaking sounds behind the thin bed curtains. They listened and heard. The sounds and noises had been scary at times—more of a fight or a duel for life. But nobody tried to run away, no one seemed hurt; they were all smiling in the morning.

Gab and Giovanna had matured quicker than the others had guessed. They learned.

Once everybody fell asleep, exploring their bodies taught them all they wanted to know. Their play in the dark started as curiosity; pleasure came as a great surprise.

For Gab, the boy—as he was then—she'd become his woman; although at that time they never had sex proper, in his eyes, she lost her virginity to him. She belonged to him.

Her father had an exact plan how those two would produce the new brilliant cadet branch of the Bernini family of actors par excellence! Those disputes he used to have with mother!

Giovanna heard her mother's voice in their fierce argument about their daughter's future, "She cannot marry Gabriel! He's her first cousin."

And father's "Stop being modern! Their children will become the crown jewels of this family!"

Then "That will never happen" of her mother's.

And his "We'll see to that!"

He planned it all well.

First, he made Gabriel drunk, telling him that Giovanna can't wait to be with him. "She will play hard to get. Don't mind that!"

He locked her in a small room, adjacent to the far-most empty stable. He pushed Gabriel in, locked the door, and ran away. He hoped that Gabe would have raped her and had to marry her!

Horrid, horrid man! And stupid, stupid, stupid! she cursed, laughing even now to her self-professed brilliant father.

Everyone knew about them being lovers for some time—except for him!

The troupe was playing in Verona when she fell for Georg. She noticed his eyes as two deep-green pools. She was lost. He was traveling with his friend but changed his plans when he saw her on stage as Isabella.

From there on, he followed the troupe. By the time they reached Adige up under the Alps, Gabriel was mad with jealousy. One night, after their performance, Gab attacked Georg who sat upfront and flirted with Giovanna all through the play, all night long.

Oh that was a scene! Gab yelled that he'll mark Georg's face to never be able to charm another girl in his life. It took all men to hold him down. She got an earful from her father afterwards. She didn't care. It was exciting to be wanted by men. She enjoyed that dangerous play like walking on a tightrope.

Giovanna, the brilliant actress, hopped down from her chaise longue with newly found vigor. She turned her eyes to the heavens. Her *Thank you* was for her Muses. Memories informed her emotions. Her eyes received the spark she couldn't find for days. When she walked on stage as Catherine that evening, she was the fire ball to respect__ she was the 'Shrew' to be tamed!

ACT III

"Are we going, Mama?"

"Of course we are going!" answered grandfather, the Count. Bent over the vast map spread on the enormous desktop he was making last changes to his trip.

That table was made-to-order, especially for this space—eight strong legs, carved to smooth lion paws, polished. The center of the library, where it stood for at least a century and half, was almost entirely taken by it.

"After your Thursday scare, I've been tempted to keep you two at home." The Countess looked up from her book.

"We wanted to surprise you with some berries," explained Louisa from her spot by the window.

"Oh, and what a surprise it was," Maria-Antonia, her mother, put the small, thin book in her lap. The deep blue silk creased around it like water around a solitary leaf.

Count could not but agree with his daughter-in-law more. "You scared us all. Such a storm!" He looked around the room. "Where's Frederik? He was just here."

Louisa was deeply sorry about the secret expedition on Thursday. She said so and immediately vanished back into her adventure, but not before she helped herself to one of small squares of marzipan pastries.

"All right, we'll all go," the Countess shook her head. She looked up at her father-in-law, "I think he's been trying his new horse."

"And we'll dance a little," said the Count and meant it. The Countess never danced with the folk unlike him. His right hand held the pointer somewhere on the map, his left extended just long enough to get to that corner piece of pastry, which was darker than the others. He popped it in his mouth and closed his eyes "Mmm, so good."

The Secret Maneuver

"We will go then? And dance?" Louisa left Robinson among the savages. "May I wear my new white dress?"

"You'll wear the folk dress I had my seamstress made for you. You needed a new trachten anyway."

"My new dirndl, that's right! I forgot about it. Where is it?"

"And no, you will not dance. You are too young."

"Oh. Why of course, Mama."

Louisa was disappointed. Her spirit slouched the way her petite body did just now. She learned new dances from a booklet that she saved her pocket money for. She was dying to try.

"It's in my dress trunk." Maria-Antonia put down her book and stood up.

"What are you reading, my dear?" Count noticed a small unfamiliar book.

The Countess picked up the thin book and stretched her arm towards her father-in-law.

"An anthology of English poetry."

Leopold took another piece of marzipan pastry and made a weak offer to his daughter-in-law. She refused as he hoped she would.

"I'll bring you some modern ones, from Weimar."

"This is—modern," she said calmly.

"But there's nothing like—"

"Sturm and drunk!" jumped in Louisa with her knowledge; a term overheard from adult conversations was surely proper here and now, she thought.

Both adults suddenly got fits of coughs. The Countess sat back and covered her face with her book; Leopold turned away and used his handkerchief to stop his laugh.

Fortunately, Louisa was more interested in her reading and tried to quickly get through the last paragraph before going upstairs. But her mother recovered too soon from her cough and was standing above her.

How does she do that? her daughter looked up.

"Put down your book. Louisa? Let's go. Now!"

Upstairs in her anteroom, painted in white with an edge of blue gentian flowers by the ceiling, the Countess rang for her maid. Soon the long, oval psyche mirror was pulled forward; the maid, mouth full of pins, was moving around Louisa, who started twirling.

"Louisa, stand still or we'll never take it in!" the Countess tried to control the fitting. She looked at her daughter through the mirror and gave a sigh.

"I thought maybe you would become more feminine by summer."

"Feminine?"

"She means 'bosoms,'" whispered the young maid to Louisa's ear as she was pining the side of her bodice.

Their faces couldn't have reacted more differently. Louisa simply opened her mouth, and the maid's face spread in a wide smile and she giggled.

"Girls?"

"Yes, Mama?"

The Countess shook her head, tilted it to the side, inspected the changes, and said, "Good. Now let's do the back."

In the servants' quarters, Magdalena closed the door and submitted to the warm air of her room. The one small window ajar couldn't help the flow up there, no matter how far the shingle roof stretched over the facade.

She spread her best clothes on the narrow bed; picking one piece after another, she started examining them with eagle sight to catch imperfections. Thomas wasn't allowed to find any on Saturday eve.

Further down the hallway, Clara—window opened, door left ajar—was undressed to her underpinnings. She looked in the windowpane.

"Not bad," she said, looking at her slightly distorted image.

All her focus was on her new blouse. It felt amazing. She was lucky that the lady's maid was her friend. Such thin cotton was out of reach for a girl like herself. What luck that the Countess didn't like how thick it was!

It was all black as is the tradition there in this part of Tyrol. She had some colorful thread, and in no time, she began embroidering sleeves with tiny stitches, assembling themselves into buttercups and bouquets of edelweiss.

Thomas will like it, Clara told herself, blushing. *It's not my fault, is it? He came at me back there, in the garden only yesterday; strong and tall.*

Clara realized how much she really liked him.

His kisses were such she'd never known had existed. She panicked at first. She thought that's what the head maid once talked about, over the feather stripping for eiderdown_ about not being a virgin anymore when a man gets inside.

I shouldn't have opened my lips! Clara crossed herself, as she sat down on the bed frame, confused. *So am I not a virgin anymore?*

She remembered seeing horses mounting mares in the field when she walked for water; field-helps were laughing at her stunned expression as she stopped to watch. Then they started calling at her, "Hey, girl! Come closer, I know how to make babies even better!"

No, it can't be like that, can it?

"Ouch!"

She pricked her finger. She was lucky the cotton was black. The little drop of her blood reminded her of something else from that girl talk. Things that happen every moon and what to do if they don't. Clara didn't hear the steps coming.

"Clara." Magdalena, Frau Ebner, was standing at the door.

"Eh?" Clara gave a start but tried to smile.

Stepping inside without slightest hesitation Magdalena said "May I go through?" just to be polite.

"Sure."

"Clara, here, hold my bodice down in the back for me, will you? I must pin the front properly_ there, all good. Looking forward to Saturday?"

"Oh yes, Frau Ebner, very."

"What are you embroidering?" Magdalena picked up the work and shook her head with expertise. "The small stitch in the middle must be tighter. I'll show you."

Not waiting for an answer, she sat down next to Clara, opened her chatelaine, and took out a fine needle.

"Hand me more thread, girl."

In a short while, Frau Ebner's skillful hand started embroidering her favorite flower in the world—the edelweiss.

Clara couldn't decide if it was generous or pushy.

Giovanna couldn't sleep. She was sitting in the loveseat in her small parlour. Her long orange and gold brocade robe crushed around her was out of place in this green painted little square room. But she had other thoughts to entertain. She poured more red into her glass.

Gab's little cousin, Carlo. As a six-year-old boy then, easily bribed with sweets, had become hers and Georg's, "billet-doux." That was a true shock for her when father presented him in Innsbruck as his witness.

That boy was a child at that time of her youth! Did he really understand German back then or has father been paying him? Little Carlo must have told Gab where she was going. Is that why he's ready to lie for her father now? Yes. Guilt. That's it.

Giovanna took a long sip from the red. It was too dry. Her lips puckered. She reached for the wax paper cone on the small white side table. Her stops at the confectioner's little store had become more frequent recently. She took out a small pink meringue and placed it between her lips; her tongue was gently tapping it until it caved and began melting in her mouth.

Georg. The last time they saw each other he gave Giovanna the most beautiful golden ring: two swallows chasing each other, never allowed to rest next to the other; she could play with it all day. She still does. That evening, decades ago, she had a premonition and asked him "Is this a partying present?"

"Of course not!" he laughed it off.

She wanted to believe anything he said. She had been secretly getting ready to elope with him. She was packed. Prepared to toss away everything she knew, all she was, all she wanted to be. She wished for one thing: to become his wife; to keep looking into his green eyes and drown in their depth. Giovana finished her wine in one gulp.

Their tight embrace was unexpectedly laced with her intuition that evening "I should go…" He didn't understand. But didn't push. They kissed one more time and she hurried away.

In a few yards she caught a glimpse of Gabriel behind the thick undergrowth.

She felt sick out of panic. Their little cousin Carlo talked!

Was it just her imagination or did the last rays of daylight bounce off a long blade? Was it his knife or the short French sword he would boast about lately?It glistened as he hurried towards Georg.

She pretended not to see him.

She knew that Georg would always wait and watch over her until she was safely on her way.

Giovanna reached for the green wine bottle and poured.

If she saw Gab, her secret lover, Georg, must have seen him as well.

Gab's vulgar shouts and angry swearing cut through the warm evening air. In a second they grew louder and louder. Georg didn't shout back. Giovanna heard the sound of two bodies colliding, muffled bodily noises of a fight. Then silence. That frightened her even more. Giovanna turned and started running.

There she saw the scene—Georg's sword and sleeve full of blood and Gabe__on the ground.

"Georg, my love!" She rushed forward to help him as his strength left him and he fell to his knees.

"Run, Giovanna, run! Leave me, please . . ."

"You are hurt! No, I won't go." Giovanna saw the two men she cared for the most and her inexperienced youth had to make a quick decision.

There was always safety in well learned lines, "You must go away now! If they find you they will—" Giovanna knew Juliet's ever since she saw her mother, Laura, in that role.

She was observing herself now as if she would watch an understudy. Her love, her fear for him was sincere yet__his "Will you help me?" came suddenly too real.

Her deep kiss sealed in all of his possible questions, and answers that she wasn't ready for.

Giovanna held her wineglass. It warmed up by her palms to the perfect temperature but she forgot to drink.

It was completely dark then by the time she found her way. She couldn't stop running until she was in the cheap inn where the troupe was lodging. It was easy to sneak in through the side door by the stables, to rush up the ladder-steep, narrow wooden staircase. Everybody was still down in the pub or outside. She went straight to bed. When the others came in, she pretended to be sound asleep.

A new day woke up, and nobody noticed that Gab vanished. They all allowed themselves to live parts of their existence as far from the others as they could. About an hour before they went on, the Principale, Marco, would walk around to inspect them all.

Not until that moment late afternoon, before their performance, had they found out about Gab. They looked in panic everywhere—they asked everyone. Gabriel Bernini was gone. All that time Giovanna kept praying. But there was no God that afternoon.

The unimaginable happened.

She saw little Carlo as he whispered something to his mother. She saw her face turned to a frightened mask. Not before she made Marco promise not to beat him she dared to repeat what little Carlo just told her.

Oh, Giovanna sees it as if it was now! Her memory was prickly like a voice singing false notes in high pitch.

She put the glass to her lips. Her eyes large with a forming memory, she sat it back untouched.

It was the next day when local fishermen found Gab down the stream. One simple small wound where his heart was. No bloody slashes. One strike.

"Murder!" Marco ran to hit Giovanna. "You whore! It's your doing! Carlo told me everything!"

"He knows nothing!"

"That sly German, the green-eyed lizard, murdered him! Can't you see!" Marco turned around. His arms spread, his palms opened in a screaming question. "You must see it! He was murdered! My Gabriel!" He sobbed and tore his shirt open.

They all were appalled. They remembered well how he reacted to his wife's tragic death. This seemed in comparison as an overblown spectacle. Marco didn't care. They didn't dare to speak nor turn and walk away.

He sent for gendarmes.

It was Georg! Can't they see it? What? Where was he from? Who were his people?

It started being too complicated. Police wanted more witnesses. Judge wanted more money. Priest wanted a contribution for a new relic. There was not even enough to pay for a proper funeral.

Giovanna's father swore vengeance. He will not stop if he has to employ some murderers himself.

Giovanna feared for her beloved. She wished him Gods' speed, closed her mind, and erased the last day with Georg from her life. She felt the ring with swallows hung low on a sash in between her breasts. She belonged to Georg forever. She'd give her life for him. Only now she understood her lines in Juliet. From now on she'd carry this feeling and enchant her audience with their truth.

Marco kept pouring salt into his open wound. He tried to trick her to make her blurt a revelation. But she was as hard and as clever as her mother. Now he saw it.

"I'll get it out of you one day!" he shouted at her right before they went to play their scene every night.

He stopped talking to her off stage. It didn't help that the others tried to make her feel better, to reason with him. In her father's eyes, it was she who was as guilty as the murderer.

It was she who killed his beloved Gabriel Bernini, the future star of European theatre houses, and she who ruined his gilded future as Gabriel's impresario.

One night, Giovanna grabbed her bundle and walked away.

No one has ever seen or heard of Georg again.

Giovanna took the glass and slowly finished her wine.

She suddenly remembered that she'd never asked him what his full name was.

The long anticipated first Saturday of summer had arrived! The Summer Dance was here!

Preparations for such an occasion were a serious matter: pieces of clothing were taken out of wooden trunks and hung out to be aired, some were traded, some made to new measurements; laces soaked in the thick sugar-water then stretched with pins on cushions to dry stiff; satin sashes carefully ironed; white embroidered knee-highs washed and whitened in a sunny spot; boots polished with a stripe of smoked pork skin; heels waxed with beeswax and sprinkled with water, rubbed with a square of chamois to the hard shine; hats brushed to even finish; red pom poms and black rooster-feathers refastened; silver pins attached.

There, the glorious parade of folks—their hopes and dreams—may begin!

Is there anything like music to let emotions out? There's nothing to match dance to make your blood rush, to warm your chest, to make your heart pound; and there's nothing like a strong drink to make heads spin and cloud one's judgement.

Musicians up high, above the floor level, were already tuning their instruments; their place behind the wooden baluster was a safe corner when eventually push and shove over a girl would happen in wee hours.

A small crowd of maids, servants, kitchen-helps, cooks, and foresters—all from the castle, as the von Schönbruck lodge was known here—just arrived. They came to mix with villagers, and some were here to meet their own family.

Women went to sit on one side, men on the other. There was still a lot of talking and drinking before the fiddler played a few notes to get everyone's attention. Then he called the first dance and turned towards his small band. Outside, the evening was slowly changing hues of blue.

With flowers above her forehead, sashes of all colors down her back, her hair braided and pinned into festoons hanging over her nape, Magdalena entered the room. She looked lovely, and she was aware of it. She expected Thomas to be there, waiting, to charge to greet her. Muffled whistles came already to welcome her there, but still no Thomas. She stood there undecided. Someone offered her beer. She shook her head No.

"I'll have some wine please,"

Clara was almost a head shorter than Magdalena. Her hair—flames on the water at sunset—were set off by a wreath of field flowers. She wore the newly embroidered black blouse, as if the wild blooms in her hair spilled and caught on her sleeves; green bodice; black skirts with a blue apron adorned with colorful sashes. Magdalena smiled at her and looked with satisfaction at her kitchen girl's outfit. There was pride in her glance; the embroidery looked amazing. She wasn't the only one who was looking.

Clara's plump body was transformed into lush curves; all of the men present noticed. A hand slipped around Magdalena's waist.

"Thomas!" she smiled broadly. "Want a sip?"

She lifted her wine glass in front of his nose.

Thomas took it and finished the red in one gulp. It made Magdalena chortle. *My man!* She thought with satisfaction.

Clarinet squeaked the first high note, and everybody—soldiers, hussars, fieldhelps, all men, and older boys—were ready to dance. In one move they slid across the room to ask women of all ages to dance now.

Magdalena got her wish; she couldn't be happier. Thomas gave her one of his wide all-teeth smiles and took her hand.

The local traditional opening dance was this long, slow number, well suited for all, the best one for any intimate conversation. Magda hoped for one like that, perhaps a surprise proclamation. Suddenly there was the change of partners. Thomas was moved up the circle. Magdalena stood face to face with an old hussar. For the rest of that dance she kept looking at Thomas. He was laughing and winking at her. She relaxed and picked up a small talk with the old horseman. When she looked up Thomas was nowhere to be found.

Hussars were there that summer; with no battles to fight, they came home to help in the fields.

There was a rare chance for a young woman to get a husband that season. One such hussar came for Clara. She was astonished by his many long thin braids. She hasn't seen them from this close ever.

He danced with gusto, strongly, leading her with certainty that felt like nothing she'd ever known. With every next spin, his eyes dark like brambles—glossy, intense—held onto her. She liked him more than she could bear. She was sure he'd come back for her again. But he went away to dance the next dance with an older woman! Clara was furious and hurt. She glanced across the room and picked the blond boy whom she turned down before. She nodded at him and he readily darted across

"This dance is mine." Thomas stepped decisively in front of the young man.

He got no argument from such a youngster. Without any question or apology, he took Clara's waist with both hands.

Music twirled through the air and pushed forth the speed. This dance didn't allow for any conversation; it was energetic and quick, but there was a lot of touching and holding tight—and even tighter if the man decided to do so.

Magdalena was standing there, hurt and puzzled. Thomas was supposed to spend all evening dancing with her. She hoped that he would let everyone know what his intentions were. Jealousy started getting hold of her. She noticed his fingers on the girl's bodice, his fingers sliding underneath, then she saw his face.

No, this can't be!

She watched him whispering in Clara's ear; and Clara laughing, tilting her head backwards. Magdalena wanted to scream, to stop this ball, to point at the redhead and shout, "Take that nasty fox maiden away!" Instead, she kept watching her hopes turning to dirt.

No, this is not going to be. I will not allow it! She can't do this to me! She can't bewitch my man and take him away! Stop her! Stop her somebody!

Old women were watching this scene with hungry curiosity, their gossip-loving tongues ready for the morsel. Magdalena couldn't stand this any longer; she turned to walk away. The music hushed. Dancers stopped in the mid movement.

The Lords of Schönbruck had arrived.

The Count, the Countess, and her two eldest children stood at the doorway, smiling, looking around. The village elders stepped forth and welcomed the noble family. The whole room took their jugs and lifted them high above their sweaty foreheads shouting "Prost! Long life and happiness to the Lords of Schönbruck!"

The Counts were well liked there; they were down-to-earth, no-nonsense lords, if eccentric at times. Count Leopold was especially loved and respected by all regardless.

Marie-Antonia, the widowed Countess von Schönbruck, smiled pleasantly, and gave a nod left and right. She was ushered to her special armchair in the head of the room; with the high, heavily carved backrest, it resembled a throne. The curtsy, which would open every dance, would be directed there. Frederik and Louisa followed her and were given two chairs not much different from the one of their mother's. They looked at each other obviously loving the special care.

The Count stayed behind among the local folks. His tricorn-hat tucked inside his tails, he lifted the pewter lid and drank his beer with gusto until he emptied the stein. A loud hurrah from the men around him greeted his bravura.

After that, musicians didn't see any reason for waiting any longer. The dance resumed with a vivid intro by the fiddler.

Thomas's arm hadn't left Clara's waist all that time; the sharp-eyed gossips had noticed. Clara had no clue. Thomas registered the prying eyes, but as any man suddenly smitten by an uncontrollable force he couldn't care less.

Marie-Antonia, Countess von Schönbruck, was dressed like every woman there—in her best trachten, the folk dress of her people. Her black blouse, black skirts, moss-green apron, all heavily embroidered just like her golden thread cap with tall black lace wings made her look like all the other married women here. When you looked closer, however, you saw no brass, no linen, no glass beads. Your eyes travelled over the over the cobweb-thin silk, resting on the many silver chatelains hanging from her waist down over her moss-green taffeta silk apron. Underneath it her black jacquard skirt was embroidered with blue gentian flowers. The large red coral earrings, like heavy drops of gold hanging from her earlobes, the many golden pins in her chignon, visible under her cap—all that splendor, heralded her social status.

There was no one to dance with. Her father-in-law made his annual kind attempt and was, as every year, politely declined. She remained distant, sipped from the glass of red, and watched.

She couldn't be disturbed from her secret— The best dancer, her Carl-Maria, his long hair tied with a black silk moireé in the back of his head, was dancing with her tonight. Her eyes held in a trance to his, to read his mind, to fulfill his wishes before the words left his full, beautiful lips under the thin mustaches.

Music came out loud again, sharply and joyfully; and fresh drinks were brought all around the room.

The Countess's lips changed into a tender smile. Dancers began choosing new partners for their next spin. Magdalena didn't wait and walked out.

"I will never forget tonight!" Louisa's voice carried brightly through the dark; her lips modeled the sound into an everlasting smile.

That year's Summer Dance seemed unexpectedly very different, and she was full of impressions.

"Did you see? Our Clara was on fire!" she marveled.

"Louisa, watch your language!"

The Countess was leading her small crowd up the hill. The waxing moon was shining brightly above them. She seemed to have sped up.

Louisa, with her chin down, turned towards her brother and whispered, "She came for you, for the ladies' choice! Ha-ha-ha, our Clara!"

He stopped and said sharply into her face, barely visible even that night, "So? She's the prettiest girl I've ever known."

He said that to hurt Louisa, and he did.

"She liked the tall hussar better than you," her whisper quickened. "She danced with him all night after our Thomas left."

Her brother's anger was palpable.

"She didn't like him!"

"Who?" asked his mother from the dark in front of him.

How does she manage to hear everything? thought her children as ever.

"No one," they replied in perfect unison, then became slightly embarrassed by that coincidence.

Frederik chose to speed up to join their mother.

The Countess smiled. Immediately a little voice came to her head, *When two quarrel, the third one smiles.*

There was a moment of quiet as the little group approached the house.

"That was some walk. I don't think we'll do it again too soon," said the Countess under her veil.

The air was full of moths, mosquitoes, and mayflies. There the first fireflies flashed their tiny lanterns through the warm summer's night. Bats high above were as busy as swallows.

Marie-Antonia turned to the servant who was carrying the lit torch for them.

"You may go back now."

The servant, whose name she'd forgotten, hesitated. He loved the Countess's voice, her manners; she was still a pretty young woman, no doubt about that. Out of reach but he liked being in her presence.

"Is there anything else?" she tried to help. No-thank you-good night__was all that he muttered and made her laugh.

His torchlight started diminishing through the dark, moving down the hill with uneven bounces as he started to jog. Music coming out the windows and all doors ajar welcomed him back. Its sound was carried all the way up to the hunting lodge. Singular bursts of laughter echoed into the quiet. The ball would be going till morning. Countess von Schönbruck started humming a dance melody. She and Carl-Maria would have danced till wee hours.

"I wish he would have walked with us," said the Countess absentmindedly out loud as she passed through the main door.

Both children turned their heads.

"Grandpa?"

But they never received an answer.

Magdalena didn't sleep a wink. Her face was like a gray kerchief which somebody ran in cold water, then squeezed all life out of it. Vertical wrinkles ran deeply through her face; by morning, she had no tears to cry. She slept briefly; violent dreams ruined even those few precious moments.

Once she appeared in the kitchen quarters, she was all dressed for the new day. Her appearance as always was meticulous; inside__ deep chaos. Her long apron was fixed with simple pins on her bodice; her hair under her cap was smoothly combed and pinned back. She was about to refresh her cheeks with a host of brief pinches to cover traces of tears.

"'Morn'," said Thomas quickly and walked in with a large basket full of wood.

There was dead silence; he was in trouble. He placed the basket by the hearth, trying not to make much noise. The silence was bursting his eardrums.

"Magdalena, c'mon it was just a dance."

The swollen bruise on his right jaw couldn't disagree more. Neither did Magdalena.

"How could you?"

She struggled not to cry. That wasn't going as she pictured it. Words more than tears started pushing forward.

Magdalena heard her voice—strange, distant, resolute. She was talking for the sake of them, them two.

She was standing there, leaning for support over the working table. Then she took out bread from its drawer, reached for the bread knife, cut a slice, then two more, put the bread back, and put the knife back; and while she kept talking, her nervous fingers were squeezing little crumbs of bread into small balls, modeling them into shapes and placing them one next to each other on the working desk.

Her emotions—a flood she couldn't block—formed into words.

In front of mesmerized Thomas, an unknown portrait of her love for him—all sacrifices she was willing to go through, to be with him in the end—was painted with monumental strokes in all colors and tones of her short, hard life.

He didn't walk away as was his first instinct when he first stepped in. He would have loved to hold her now.

Only that his body was still carrying the scent of Clara. He wore a fresh shirt that morning. His hair combed with unusual effort. Magdalena must have guessed already. He didn't step forward to offer her his opened arms.

"So this is the end of us?" was not a question Magdalena posed to herself—a mere observation of someone with common sense and brightness of thoughts.

She looked at him. Thomas didn't seem awake enough from the weight of alcohol yet. His eyes were not there; his arms were folded in a tight embrace across his broad chest.

An armor against my embrace! thought Magdalena but didn't move.

She was looking at him. There he was—everything she'd ever wanted!

She would get him back, she knew it. But it will never be as it was before. She knew herself too well. She too folded her arms now.

"We need more wood."

A kitchen help came in and asked, "Is Clara here? I need help with marking eggs."

"She's picking fresh parsley in the small garden. I'll send her," Magdalena answered without looking at the girl.

It was all a lie. She hadn't seen the redhead that morning at all.

"Go fetch some bacon in the back larder," Frau Ebner ordered.

Thomas turned toward Magdalena.

"Lena, it was nothing. It means nothing. She's just a little fox."

"Who?"

"Clara."

"Thieves."

"What?"

"Foxes. They are thieves. They take anything they come across—eggs, meat, berries, anything. One has to lay down heavy traps_or_" she took out the butcher's knife.

Thomas didn't have to listen to this. He turned and walked out to another hot summer day.

The kitchen-help coming from the larder saw him leaving and shook her head "Poor Frau Ebner."

She walked in the kitchen and placed the package on the working table.

"Here's the bacon. Should I go help Clara?"

Magdalena wasn't thinking about eggs and her "Yes, yes" was just a way to get the girl out of there.

Magdalena kept holding the knife with such ferocity that all her knuckles turned pale. She shoved it back to its block. Her wrist hit the small cup with a last gulp of water left in it. It was like a metaphor of life—one inconspicuous movement and it spills it all out to the last drop.

Thomas belongs to me, as God is my witness! I will make it right again. A dangerous idea started forming in Magdalena's head. She needed to ask someone old and wise. Her confessor was too young. That always bothered her. She couldn't clasp her hands, close her eyes, and tell him her secrets, expecting wisdom and understanding.

"Look at him! He's barely out of the seminary!" she would always say.

The help walked in.

"I don't think Clara marked any eggs at all. It's all there, untouched."

Magdalena took the girl with her as a witness, and they ran to the servant quarters.

Without a single knock, Frau Ebner burst into Clara's room.

The bed wasn't slept in.

There was nothing to tell what was going on. They ran outside calling Clara's name. Then Thomas's. He came in a jiffy from the workshop, still holding a sickle, the one Magdalena asked him to fix a month ago.

"Did she run away?" asked the young kitchen help without scruples. They didn't have answers.

Magdalena breathed heavily; her hands trembled. When she caught her breath, she made her decision. It traveled through the kitchen and up to the house. They would wait. This was not going to disturb the life in the main house. Magdalena was in charge. It was final.

Once lunch was cooked and, after church, carried to the main house, Magdalena sat down at her working desk. She took out a quill, sharpened it, and went to the niche for the inkwell. It used to be her mother's, carved from a cherrywood into a short branch with two peaches and leaves. The actual glass inkwell was inserted in one of the fruits. Magdalena caressed the smooth orb of the carved peach.

Paper was in a tin box with a green lid in the tall cupboard. Her hand was heavy, unskillful. She couldn't make a mistake—paper was scarce. Her lips vanished, pressed together over her teeth, squeezed into a thin line. Focused on every line, she requested a private talk with the Count. She couldn't risk losing it and took her letter herself to the valet.

Later in the day the answer came back for Frau Ebner: Herr Count was too busy and would talk to her before he leaves tomorrow morning.

So that was that. Not even Leopold could help her. She was alone again. But she would find the way out of their predicament. She had the strength. She would have her way. She always does.

Monday! First bird calls drew the curtain of the day. Everything was packed: The last three letters from Johann Wolfgang in Leopold's pouch. His meerschaum safely in the deep inner pocket.

Just like before every trip, he was excited. This time he was more than slightly anxious. He tried to push away the real purpose of his trip. An echo of fear flew through his stomach. No, he must not start fleeing!

Time of peace didn't necessarily mean that travel was safe from highway robbers. But then, he never traveled unarmed. It was natural that he took a larger entourage this time around. He would be taking Franz. There would be two footmen, together with two coachmen. They were a strong group with twelve pistols total. All former soldiers before they joined the Count's household, after he bought them out from the army. Good men—strong and reliable.

Provisions were being packed; he could see Thomas and his helpers walking back and forth.

Count shook his head.

Poor Magdalena. What is her note about? Leopold held the paper, still folded, unsealed, in his hand. *But surely, she didn't object to Thomas's dancing with that little redhead? She never does.*

Count tossed the paper on his desk. Magdalena. *She has a soft spot for him. She never turns away when he brushes her breasts with the back of his palms in a narrow doorway. That woman takes everything in slow stride, philosophically, with stoicism—that's her nature. Even keel. She sent me a message through Franz that she'd like to talk with me.*

Before my trip? No. That will have to wait. He started feeling the pressure of time. He wanted to be far away as quickly as possible.

His daughter-in-law was now the mistress in charge. She would deal with that kitchen business.

He was dressing in a hurry; old Johann couldn't keep up with him.

"Johann, you will have some good slow days when I am up north," said the Count.

Johann kept fixing Leopold's garters; it suddenly occurred to the Count that his old valet couldn't hear him.

ACT IV

"What now?"

Count von Schönbruck wasn't ready to slow down. They were on the last leg of their trip.

Early morning was cloudy; they left the inn at dawn to get to Weimar before dark. A messenger appeared from nowhere.

The man checked the coat of arms on the coach and compared it with the one on the letter and shouted, "A letter for Leopold Count von Schönbruck!"

His horse was dancing in place, mincing his nervous steps.

The Count pulled so hard on his steed's tender mouth that the animal went on his hinds and hopped to the side. He prayed that his men didn't notice fear that overpowered his face. He was tired, too vulnerable.

"From Countess von Schönbruck!" announced the messenger.

Leopold had neither time for a message nor any willingness to accept one. The horseman saluted and handed him an envelope. It had two seals—one of his own coat of arms, the other one of the young Countess, his daughter-in-law.

She just can't be left alone, can she? the Count sighed. *No. Whatever that is, that will have to wait. Nothing could stop me, especially now after five days' journey.*

"No reply!" the Count shouted from his saddle.

The messenger's hand flew to his hat one more time, he turned his horse and galloped away.

Leopold tucked the letter inside the double front of his jacket and forgot about it. With light impatience, he kicked the freshly combed, glossy chestnut sides of the noble animal. They shot forward, leading the way to Weimar.

Elizabeth von Witanovski

Marie-Antonia, Countess von Schönbruck, opened her eyes. For a second, she couldn't remember where she was. She stayed in that safe place between dream and reality for a second longer. She must have dozed off. Slightly embarrassed, she glanced around.

It was still early morning. Warm breeze started coming in through the French doors playfully meandering fine translucent curtains. Flies were buzzing with an effervescent crescendo, fighting for the best morning sunny spot on the warm wooden window frame.

She hadn't been sleeping well ever since her father-in-law left for Weimar.

She was alone there with her children when that horrid business with the redhead girl came around. She had dispatched a letter to the Count immediately. He wrote back only a month later.

Poor girl was stabbed. She was so young. They buried her all in white. A vagabond, they said. She was a foolish girl to go with a stranger down to the river. *Naïve, stupid!* They didn't even call any officials to come up there. Frau Ebner said that it was so clear to everyone that a ruffian was involved.

She has common sense, Magdalena. The Countess tried to remember how she came to their household. Was it before she, Marie-Antonia, married into this family? *It's so much easier that way. She's a treasure. Yes. No officials, no disturbance.* Marie-Antonia despised funerals.

Foolish girl. Thoughtless. Selfish!

She closed the book she had been trying to read. Her needlework frame had a new piece of Indian cotton attached to it. Her eyes narrowed. She started visualizing the new embroidery. *Times after war or time between wars? Dangerous times. Have there ever been any other ever?*

The Countess surely liked her sudden position in the helm of the household but not with challenges like that one!

Simple girl. No noble girl would have dreamed doing something like that! Countess reached for the round reed basket. Under its lid was a collection of rare silk yarns. Slim fingers enjoyed the colorful touch. She chose several and stopped again.

She felt so sorry for Frederik. He seemed to be infatuated with that girl, *Clara, right?* The village ball was his first adult dance. She was very pretty. Men were always swarming around her. She would have indeed obliged had the countess asked her to be the first for Frederik. Such a girl surely had experiences that would make a noble woman blush.

Too late now. Stupid girl! Ruined all the fun for him! He really liked her.

Oh, was the young Count difficult to console when they found her. She thought he would be ill again.

But that was already so long ago. *Why bring it back?* She took a long breath through her slightly turned-up nostrils and closed the little basket. She hung the selected yarn on the frame, and pulled her blue cashmere shawl over her shoulders. Red-and-orange arabesques of the woven pattern were like exotic fruits. She smiled and rang the small brass bell.

Women going down to the river for water were singing outside. She heard one of the field-helps teasing them—their giggles and sharp-tongued answers and more giggles.

Trees were full of silky leaves. Flowers in rich colors as if showing off their palette to inspire the trees__The perfect mid-September day.

"Bring me some hot chocolate—no, wait! I'll have just some apples and plums with honey, ask Magdalena if we have hazelnuts already," the Countess ordered.

She heard Louisa commanding her younger brothers somewhere out of sight, down on the lawn, under the terrace probably. She looked outside and decided to sit on the balcony.

There was a knock on the door, and it opened immediately.

"I'm outside!" Countess, sitting in her wicker love-seat called from under her sun umbrella. The plate with fruit she ordered was brought in. She dismissed the girl and picked up a small paring knife balancing on top of the fruit in the bowl. Its handle was carved in bone. She couldn't remember seeing it before. As she slowly turned it in her fingers, her mind put the pieces of that image together—a young woman under branches of oak leaves, dressed in the folk dress of Tyrol, with a knife in her heart.

The Countess picked a few hazelnuts from the plate. None were ever as sweet as the new crop. *September already.*

She saw Frederik, splendid up in the saddle. He was trying his new horse, an exquisite Arab steed, under the careful eye of her riding master. The Countess could hear Frederik's laughter as the horse took to galloping in the manège, the circle of sand. She was looking at him with pride. He surely was a talented horseman like his father.

He was a talented fencer too like his father used to be. His death was still puzzling to everybody.

Marie-Antonia's face turned inward; she let her chin almost touch the large cameo on her pearl necklace.

She knew that her father-in-law was right, but he had expected her to accept his judgment easily. She saw that too but was slow to admit that what Fred possessed in dexterity, he lacked in maturity_ her euphemism for intelligence.

What was needed now and quickly was a good, educated tutor. Since her father-in-law wasn't keen on answering her correspondence, she arranged everything on her own without consulting him. The tutor she chose from a handful of recommendations was on his way. His name was Tristan.

Tristan let go of the book cover. The thick leather, embossed with his family coat of arms, dropped down. It closed his thoughts with a heavy thud. His white hands carefully fixed the brass buckles attached to the leather belts on each side.

He remained standing in front of the low book-holder, pensive, unsatisfied with his days of research of his family tree.

There was not much about his mother—not much about other women in general, except for his great-grandmother. But then, she was the richest woman of Lower Austria of her time.

The noble wives were entrusted to bear children to their husband's family, to propagate the family tree. They were expected to do so until they were too old or died during childbirth or, after giving birth too many times, closed their eyes forever in eternal relief.

When the grave news about his own mother's untimely death reached him at the university, he cried for the void she'd left him to deal with. He mourned the time they had never spent together. He felt angry for the blank spots in his memory that she'd never felt necessary to fill.

He knew absolutely nothing about her feelings for him or the others. She had neither given any valuable observations nor had she volunteered any advice.

She died exhausted before he could ask her pressing questions about daily life, relationships, about the complex puzzle of love. He didn't know anything about her wishes, her hopes, what colors she loved, what books, what songs.

Tristan realized that he should have asked his eldest brother. He must have known her like none of the eight siblings did. He was the single surviving child for eight years. Tristan wiped his eyes and blew his nose. It was too late now—his brother was gone. This was a cry over spilled milk.

Tristan was all dressed for his journey: Yellow deerskin pants, tied under his knees by two pairs of leather garters; silver buckles; and gray cotton socks tucked in his high black riding boots. Dark blue chintz jacket with metal buttons under his long canvas duster. Black hat with wide brim. He pulled up the cuff of his long yellow leather glove. His fine linen shirt had his initials embroidered white on white along the third button from top. Its collar was touching his cheeks, white necktie underneath wound five times around, until it was fixed in the middle by a golden pin. The pin was an enameled version of Tristan's personal coat of arms—a parting present from his eldest brother. The something-to-remember-me-by. His brother left to fight in America. Tristan had not heard from him ever.

"Your horse is ready, sir."

"Oh yes." Tristan started navigating his digits through the second of his travel glove's tall wide sleeve.

"Is father in the garden?"

"No, sir."

The young stable boy looked down on the red brick–paved ground somewhere in front of Tristan's riding boots;

His voice sounded a little flat as he said quickly, "Herr Baron left early to town."

Tristan exhaled sharply. *What a relief!*

"Good," he said as he pressed the wide-brimmed hat deeper and fastened the duster's top hook.

His travel bag was tied behind on the saddle; it was full of provision for his one-day trip. He placed his left leg into the prepared arm-formed step and pushed up from the stable boy's hands. This little moment of being airborne was among Tristan's favorites. To fly! To soar! And never come back!

Up in the saddle, he bent forward and whispered a few words into his horse's mane. They were two friends about to take a long uncertain trip.

Tristan's left fingers touched his felt hat just out of habit; there was no one to say goodbye to. His thighs squeezed glossy white sides of his well-fed animal. Like a singular barge on a quiet, undisturbed lake early in the morning, his horse started trotting towards the unknown.

The young Countess looked to the Alps framing the horizon. She saw all the hues of blues on blue. Thick gray clouds mixed with those thin ones, which resembled white feathers, were gathering around the highest peaks. She knew it would rain in less than a day.

She looked across the park and the vast meadow bordering with the alley of ancient trees. Everywhere she looked was a story or a fragment of emotion she and her husband started creating together—this house, the park, their five children—which they never had a chance to finish.

Her darling Carl-Maria was killed on the battlefield; he died a heroic death fighting an enemy soldier, man to man, she was told. She'd never stopped listening for the sound of his horse, the familiar jingling of his saber hung from his baldric. Sunlight would reflect off the golden ropes of his high hat, glistened off the black eye-shield. *His epaulets would glitter, little lights flickered under his chin.* She never even forgot how straight he sat on his steed, the short overcoat with brown fur collar over his shoulder. *Oh, those many, many braids bouncing around his beloved head!*

He would lift his arm and call from far away her name. It was a short, sweet ritual—their intimate hello. Only after that would he nudge his horse into full gallop, harness jiggling, horseshoes hitting the ground, their loud clicking in the courtyard shortly afterward. She would have recognized that sound among thousands. She never stopped listening for it.

She took to her pen; she must find solace in her diary. She opened on the new page; the penholder was her closest helper. It inevitably ended between her lips as usual, since forming a sentence wasn't something she could do easily.

Louisa darted through the library door.

"I just needed to check something!"

Her mother glanced up at her from the anteroom.

"Why of course."

There was her first surviving girl: happy, beautiful, curious, intelligent. She had all the advantages a young woman of her social standing could wish for. Her prospects were one of the finest.

She's not going to remain a little girl for much longer, the Countess thought, observing more with curiosity than sadness.

It occurred to her that the time to start thinking about Louisa's marriage had arrived.

Louisa climbed up the wooden spiral of the library steps, carved from one piece of an ancient walnut tree. She moved out a thin volume bound in leather, embossed all around with Greek key pattern in gold.

Several moments later, her heart pounding from speeding, Louisa dropped on the carpet in her bedroom. She was lying there looking at the low ceiling. All of a sudden, the bright white paint was no longer blank: complex images and pieces of memories that were not even truly hers colored the rectangle above. She turned and sat up on her heels; her mind was already filling up the pristine paper.

Words were pouring out of her mind. She wasn't certain what was a dream and what was the truth, but it felt wonderful to put all her emotions to words! When she finished writing, she closed the book and sat on it.

Louisa looked towards the small mantel clock when horseshoes clicked in the courtyard where a horse made a loud, wet sound through his snout. Then all stopped for a second. The brief silence was at once overpowered by new sounds and noises.

She heard first servants rushing out and excited voices of her siblings.

Suddenly, a timbre of an unknown voice pleasantly reached her room—their new tutor just arrived!

She heard their mother's kind greetings; there was joy and cheer in all that cacophony. Louisa was looking for her slippers. Why does she always kick them off?

Fred's voice, distorted by his anger, cut loudly into the calm afternoon.

"I thought he was coming for me? Only for me!" he demanded to know.

The jolly day was left trampled on the cobblestones; the loud stumping of Frederik's boots was making practically a rhythmical pattern as he was marching angrily away, it made Louisa giggle.

Oh, Fred!

She knew that it won't last—the anger, the tutor. Some patterns seemed to be woven tightly into his life like the patterns in Persian carpets covering floors of this lodge.

In the end, Mother realized her mistake—Frederik had Tristan only for himself.

She hired a new governess, and life went on as it used to be.

In the last weeks of summer, the young Countess was all packed for her yearly pilgrimage to Salzburg to see her family friend, the bishop. This time, she was meeting him in her family chapel. Her family coat of arms above the gold and ebony altar was being renovated, and she wanted to see for herself. She sent money for it to be re-gilded.

She received a letter from her father-in-law about his intentions to move to Burgenland. The altar would be perfect at Christmas time all decorated with green and red. She will see it next year.

Magdalena had the coach packed high with baskets of breads, strudels and pies, and apples carefully set in straw, as were jars of jams that the Countess requested for her trip.

How wonderful to have such a capable woman around, the Countess thought. *She's a housekeeper and knows about many other things.*

The Countess forgot all about the previous housekeeper. *Was she an unpleasant woman! She couldn't stay under one roof with her for long!* Now, how did Magdalena come to the von Schönbrucks? As usual, she dismissed the rumor about Carl-Maria and Magdalena with one word_ *Preposterous!*

Her mind was already miles away. The family's upholstered coach was ready. Two footmen in the back of her coach and her maid beside the coachman were up in the seat.

She waved to her children assembled in the courtyard. There were nannies and Tristan, the new tutor, with Frederik at his side. He's capable. Not without problems; like his complaint about Frederik's slow progress! Such disappointment. Perhaps Frederik will find himself in horsemanship, saber fights.

Of course, she knows that Fred is a bit_dim. The army would be the best choice for him. She intended to let him have some fun before the uniform and strict orders alter his life.

She was happy about her choice. The rough start behind the relationship of those two seemed to have taken a new direction.

Marie-Antonia, Countess von Schönbruck, leaned back to spread all over the lush cushions. For two and a half days, she doesn't have to make one single decision about her household. She looked at her hands and started playing with her rings. Then she cuddled up in the eiderdown, encased in soft yellow satin, and fell asleep.

"Tristan! Wait for me!"

"You had plenty of time to get ready. Speed up now!"

"I'll tell on you!"

"Tell what? That you were not listening? Your mother's first command was to teach you discipline—in *everything*, I mind you."

Frederik was crimson red in the face as he was trying to get his arm back into the jacket and handle textbooks and his rucksack.

"Where are we going?"

"Not too far. Just to the waterfall to recite some poetry!"

"Poetry?" Fred managed to put his rucksack over his jacket. "Not about nature?"

Tristan started pacing up the hill with more vigor than Frederik could match.

Suddenly he heard the waterfall. It made him curious. He hadn't been up there this year yet. Behind the last spruce trees—there it was__in its full magnificence! Its deafening sound was like all the church bells on big Friday!

Tristan didn't give up, not even here.

"What's wrong with poetry?"

Frederick looked at him with pain in his face.

"I will not need it in the army!"

Tristan decided not to hear that.

"Recite some for me."

"I don't remember, they were all so dull," Fred scoffed.

"Dull?" repeated Tristan and squatted down to his rucksack.

Over the sound of the falling waters, his voice came bright and strong:

> In spreading mantle to my chin concealed,
> I trod the rocky path, so steep and gray,
> Then to the wintry plain I bent my way
> Uneasily, to flight my bosom steel'd.
> But sudden was the newborn day reveal'd:
> A maiden came, in heavenly bright array,
> Like the fair creatures of the poet's lay
> In realms of song. My yearning heart was heal'd.
> Yet turn'd I thence, till she had onward pass'd,
> While closer still the folds to draw I tried,
> As though with heat self-kindled to grow warm;
> But follow'd her. She stood. The die was cast!
> No more within my mantle could I hide;
> I threw it off,-she lay within mine arm.

The nearby waterfall took care of sound in the moments of silence like the one that followed.

Frederik was standing there, looking at Tristan in awe.

With a bow, his tutor added, "Johann Wolfgang Goethe, 'The Friendly Meeting.'"

Then without paying any further attention to his pupil, the tutor took out a waxed cloth parcel with wedges of bread and speck.

The oval metal cup attached to his rucksack was for a drink. He climbed up the nearest steep slope to get fresh water from the spring.

It took Frederik an extra few moments to process what just happened. His senses were overpowered by this magical place. Rhythm of poetry. Revelation he had been steering away from. He couldn't think why he thought Louisa's little poems silly. They had rhythm. He's never felt words with such intensity flooding his body.

Every pore, every breath. He looked around. His face permeated with brightness like never before. His eyes were clear dew drops. Fragrance of wild flowers by his feet, herbs climbing up high on the rocks. Sunshine filtered through layers of greens and blues of the dense woods. Frederik was in love.

Leopold, Count von Schönbruck, sat in the salon of Goethe's protector—the home of the duke's clever mistress, to be precise. Leopold was trying to follow, to be part of conversation, the way he would always be. But somehow his usual bravado, unlike in his letters—composed over several days, even weeks at a time—lacked the quick wit of his earlier days.

He sat there, still an enthusiastic observer, but not keen on brainy language, although his opening ideas remained as fine as ever. The difference was not his age—Leopold didn't come to Weimar for sophisticated conversation; he was there to hide.

His secret mission, which nobody was aware of, altered his days there more than he wished to admit. His senses on alert gave him a sudden unexpected distance. His focus was on himself.

It brought him a sharp view of the social landscape. He saw this gathering with fresh eyes. He was reminded of what Wolf told him ahead: the inspired Duke Carl-August of Weimar and his fits of anger but brilliantly gifted in arts, observer and supporter. Leopold observed that this von Herder—"the Priest," as Leopold named him for his own private use—was unpleasant and pushy.

He was certainly harsh. His ambivalent judgement of this small group as provincial and oppressively cosmopolitan seemed to the Count as professional jealousy. As an old friend, he felt he had special rights as far as Johan-Wolfgang was concerned. He felt irritated towards Schiller, the newcomer, the star. Leopold couldn't hide it.

He felt better back in Goethe's house, especially in the Juno room, where the enormous several-foot-tall head of the Greek goddess's statue stood on a pedestal presiding over the impossibly small room. He'd sit with Wolfgang listening to his reading from his new writings. He was amazed how much his friend's capacity for storing information evolved. His inspirational, inquisitive, analytic mind and his curiosity for everything new to be examined, to be introduced to the public—those were Leopold's favorite moments. Until recently.

Surrounded by collections of minerals, fossils, shells of sea crustaceans, coral branches, Wolf picked one specimen and held it in front of Leopold's green eyes, "Remember?"

"What?" Leopold took the stone from Goethe's fingers. It was a small boulder of uninteresting grays and browns.

"I picked it above Adidge"

Leopold forgot to smoke. His friend noticed. "Poldi, you look as if you just bit into a rotten plum!"

He teased Leopold further and took the stone from him. "Was she worth staying behind? Was she full of surprises?" he pulled the round rock apart "Like this?"

Leopold refocused. There were glittering red garnets inside the shabby pod.

"No, there was no treasure." He didn't wish to say *there has been nothing but trouble!* He had no intention to start a conversation he ran away from in Innsbruck.

The clever built-in cabinets holding collections of engravings and prints suddenly lost their glow.

In the upcoming months Wolf would read sketches of his autobiography *Dichtung & Warhelt*, or *Poetry & Truth*, looking up at times when he touched on details from their youth.

"You don't mind this, Poldi, do you?" Wolf would ask.

In the heart of his home, Goethe was Leopold's old friend Wolf who seemed to have a ready opinion on everything and allowed his old friend to present his. He held no judgment, just joy from conversations. There they could laugh and argue about the silliest things which were not waiting for anybody's approval. There they didn't have to be brilliant, although Leopold thought that Wolf was always brilliant without exception. They could smoke and sip different wines while forming ideas which were not judged by a crowd of eager followers. Wolf dropped the whole Adidge story. Leopold was able to breathe freely again.

Here, Christianne ruled, and their little son walked around in his long baby dress with a thick bumper around his still-fragile head.

This was the oasis Leopold needed and which was offered to him generously—all the treasures tangible and ephemeral he could have ever wished for. The closest circle included some handsome ladies, still young but not naive, who recognized charms Leopold almost forgot he had. His other life seemed far away. Only then he relaxed into fun, which kept presenting itself daily and forgot all about his fear.

Marie-Antonia was lying in bed in her small, green painted bedroom in the Schönbruck family's townhouse in Innsbruck. She remained motionless, her eyes wide open. The tall, white tile stove in the corner was still breathing warmly.

She hurried back home from her trip to Salzburg, citing poor health. She went straight to bed and didn't want to see anyone until she sent for them.

It was very early when she rang for her maid. She asked to take some fruit, tea, butter biscuits, and some honey in her room.

Once the door closed, she crossed the room and sat down at her desk. She took out her diary from its hiding niche. It had been sitting there for years—empty, lifeless.

How she wished she didn't travel this year. But it was fate. She knew it now.

Marie-Antonia, Countess von Schönbruck, opened the booklet with impatient speed. She pressed down on its stiffened pages to flatten them down.

Her quil started running up and down the pages, placing down her emotions quicker than she could process her thoughts. Her pen briefly flew down to the inkwell, as if in fear that it might lose her speed.

She was finally getting rid of what she had been keeping to herself for all those days now—locked deeply inside with shame, unable to cry, unable to scream.

Always to be composed for the old Count's sake, for the children's sake, for the family's name. That stopped right now. She was ready to see it all written. Her thoughts were flying like dark storm clouds.

> ...I was in the park by the path when I saw the messenger. My heart stopped. I saw my husband's coat-of-arms on the saddle bag. The man I knew well, my husband's squire, jumped from the horse as he saw me, ran, and knelt in the dust to hand me an envelope. "Madame," the letter said, "your husband had died in early hours, heavily wounded by an enemy, in a close, man-to-man sword fight."
>
> When I woke up in my bedroom, my nurses and my doctors were all there. But I didn't go to labor. I went numb. Our little girl was born when her time was right, a little crumb, without a father—the hero who was killed in the battle.
>
> My hero, Carl-Maria. My darling husband. The exclusive secret maneuver failed him inexplicably. For the first time in the family history. We've been mourning him since.

A few weeks ago, I travelled to Salzburg, as I do every year. The Bishop is an old family friend. The place has other family ties, mine and my husband's.

I always have to dress my best when I go there. They are all snobs.

My veil down over my face in such a dusty square, I started walking with my maid when the door of an inn opened and out fell two drunken soldiers—at midday, mind you!

They were trying to outdo each other in sort of accomplishments. I stopped, frightened they would trample me to the ground. I watched and overheard their shouts.

When I came to, I was surrounded by a small crowd. My maid was holding me on her lap. My mind came to as quickly as I did, and I wished I did not.

Now I had a secret which I didn't ask for—a horrid secret. For from what the men were shouting at each other, I learned that my husband didn't die on the battlefield, that he didn't die a "heroic death for his Emperor," as the official letter put it.

No, he went to fight over a woman, and they fought with broken bottles! Over a whore! He's dead because he wasn't quick enough! Now I understand that it was that woman's kerchief that was enclosed with the letter saying, "This was on his heart." They thought, naturally, that it was mine. He'd laid with a whore! Not a hero but a . . . a . . .

Countess stopped writing. She could not make herself find a word which could fit what she was feeling.

She bent forward and rested her head on the cool edge of the green marble top. She didn't try to stop her sobs. She neither lifted her hand to wipe her burning eyes nor stop streams of hot, sticky tears dripping straight down, sinking into the dark red carpet among the forget-me-nots blue of the Turkish patterns.

When she finally rang for her maid, it was late afternoon.

The young woman arrived and met with a woman she'd never known before—quick, smiling, capricious.

It all rang false, but the young girl was not experienced enough to notice.

"My bright blue dress today and my turquoise hair pins." said her mistress in a high-pitched melodious voice.

The maid was standing there, hesitant what to do with the mauve dress—the one with gray mourning laces she was holding over her forearm.

Her mistress grew impatient, "Move!"

The maid's eyes glistened with tears. She had never been yelled at by her lady before. But it was not the end of the sudden change.

"Stop staring, girl! It's time to live a little."

Countess turned towards the looking glass and took down the black veil hung over its gilded frame for those last five years. She tossed it on the floor. Her maid was uncertain what to do next.

Her mistress crossed to the ebony trunk and took out her favorite white lace shawl. With particularity unknown to her maid, she arranged it on the mirror frame herself.

There!

Her hands picked up the black piece of silk from the floor and wound it up into a tight ball. She handed it to the shocked girl.

"Here. Do whatever you wish with it. I don't want to see it ever again."

Then she had yet another thought.

"Wait!" cried the Countess.

Her mouth almost gave way to a broad smile when she thought, *Let's just get rid of the past right now!*

She opened the bottom drawer of the polished black cherrywood chest and took out an embroidered handkerchief. Only now she noticed that it had a cypher *G* embroidered in one corner.

"Here, take this one too!"

Her maid was hesitant if that truly were what her mistress wanted and waited one moment too long.

"Go! What are you waiting for? Toss them, burn them, or whatever!"

Before her maid even closed the door, Marie-Antonia stepped towards the newly decorated looking glass and sat down. She saw her face clearly for the first time in years. She still looked young. She'd forgotten how young.

She moved forward and looked closer, eyes to eyes at herself.

"Yes," she whispered through unstoppable tears," It's about time."

Louisa gave a sigh. So it was decided—Fred is going to be a cadet.

He wasn't in a hurry when he was leaving. He held her very close when it was time for him to go. She couldn't remember the last time he hugged her that tight.

Military. Mother said that he loved that prospect, Louisa thought, certain that he would look dashing in his hussar uniform.

She told him. He winked at her. It made her blush for no reason!

The time was standing still or it felt that way, more than ever before. Younger siblings couldn't make her enjoy their games for the first time. She walked away from some of their favorite games. They stopped looking for her. Louisa felt lonely. With Grandpapa in Weimar, this would positively be the longest autumn. She missed them all already.

I'll write letters to him, that's it! the young Countess decided. *I'll write to him about everything!*

She placed a small aquarelle of Weimar, which her grandfather painted, in front of her. There was a small group of hikers in the foreground in ridiculous clothes of times long gone. Above each of them her grandfather wrote their names: "Goethe, me . . ."

Louisa smiled and, instead of writing, started walking around the wall. One aquarelle next to each other; there were some small landscapes with or without travelers, sheets of paper depicting interiors, an unusual small square painting with a circle of colors, another similar one, and then a room with an enormous head of a Greek goddess.

Louisa remembered the correspondence. Now it was easy to start with a question:

Who is that enormous head, Opa?

And although she knew from her mother that when Opapa travels, he was not keen on corresponding, she sat down to write anyway.

"My guess is," she wrote with absolute sincerity, "that the house is tall and was built around the full body of that gigantic, magnificent statue, like the house built around the large tree that we saw up in the mountain!"

There was freedom in knowing Opa would never ridicule any of her ideas.

"Am I right, O_?" She felt suddenly like calling him Leopold instead of Opa.

All windows ajar, the book he was reading stayed abandoned in his lap. Leopold was looking into the warm light of another midday. Another spring with friends, surrounded by the lush scent of gardens underneath the windows, the fragrance of roses and peonies, the sweetness of pine trees in bloom. Count felt fear. He knew well what triggered it. Fear on several levels. All of them possible venues to a disaster.

He noticed a man following him through Weimar open market. He could have been mistaken; but his reason told him that he wasn't. Secret Police? A private investigator? It was nowadays a modern thing to do.

It was easy to find out where he went. Quido knew. His people in *The Blatt* probably too. That meant all of Innsbruck was well informed. Quido's informants came to mind. Shady characters.

This was too much for such a bright day. Leopold decided to take a swim. The shallow river running the length of the garden was warm and inviting. He needed to clean his body and mind.

When he came back from his swim, all wrapped up in his Turkish bathrobe, he sat down on the terrace to smoke one of his friend's small white Dutch clay pipes. His face was pensive; his green eyes looked more inside than out through the landscape of the park.

"Are you homesick?" a friendly voice asked from the garden under him.

He grinned back at his friend Wolfgang's companion, Christianne. Her almost-black eyes, like two drops of ink, smiled at him. The dimples under her high cheek bones moved up. She had become a friend—wise, nonjudgmental. Yet he wouldn't have admitted his fear, nor would he speak the truth about his youth, not even to her. And so he reached for the first available half truth.

"I feel restless."

He looked suspiciously at her. She chose not to notice.

"Then you should try to write again." She was the only one besides Wolfgang who knew about this ambition of his youth.

How much does she know from Wolf about me and about my past? How much does Wolf remember? Leopold was unable to recall if he ever told him about Giovanna being in Innsbruck at all. Decades ago was the last time when Wolf shook his head in friendly disagreement before they parted in Italy.

"I think I am more homesick than I realized."

Christianne brushed her forehead with the back of her palm. One of her dark curls bounced back. She tried to tuck it under the broad, blue ribbon.

"Then you should ask yourself how long will all these diversions here sustain you for."

She wasn't a highly educated woman, but her mind was quick and her knowledge vast. Her reason worked straight to the point. Hers was common sense and a bright outlook of the world. Maybe that's what Wolfgang valued in her the most. Her full figure, from Leopold's viewpoint from the top, above her, was a composition of pleasant curves and arabesques. What a sumptuous, statuesque build, Count von Schönbruck thought. She was delightful.

Her brother was a well-respected writer; the town society fussed about him. She was too unconventional—they had rejection and sneer for her. An unmarried woman living freely with a man!

Leopold surprised himself by thinking with sudden doubt, *Freely? When they talk about her brother, he is the talented one, the man from an important town of Weimar. When they talk about her, the town changes size and importance. They call her "that village woman."*

Leopold observed with surprise that even the Schillers followed the suit.

Freedom of an unmarried woman. Like Magdalena. The count stood up abruptly. *What did Frau Ebner want to talk to me about before this trip? It was an unpleasant business with Clara. Murdered. Now, with the redhead out of her way, she will have Thomas for herself no doubt.*

An alarming image flashed through his mind. It brought back the stream of fear. What women do, what they are capable of should have remained a mystery to him. Too late for that! As usual, his thoughts meandered on their own. There was again Giovanna—another unmarried woman.

With all his will Leopold tucked fears away and left the study to write a letter.

Herr Marschalek couldn't believe the sudden twist of the slow Bernini case.

Not many people knew that Judge Gotschalk was an honest man, intelligent with exceptional curiosity and a natural gift for detection and analysis.

It took only a few interviews of the Bernini troupe for him to see the clear picture.

His questions were calm and inconspicuous, leaving the people sitting in front of him in the fragile modern, black chair wondering what he meant by his examination.

He recognized that there was more to this old so-called murder case. The man with a lot of money made the mistake that the judge has seen repeatedly throughout his career as a man of law.

Marco Bernini, inherited a fortune from a Countess in Italy. He fell into a trap of thinking that from now on he's granted invisibility.

Fascinated, Judge Gotschalk listened to Giovanna's story about her mother Flora, her quarrels with Marco, her husband, and her sudden, unexplainable death. His immediate change of Flora's original plans.

The judge was making quick notes with his left hand, sipping from a full glass of water.

When he finished, he looked at Giovanna. She smiled and the bright vision excited him against his will. He did with his feelings what he did with the sheet of his document—placed it on top of several more in green leather folders.

The confessions of the actors sounded like one voice. They all agreed about the circumstances of Flora Bernini's death, about Marco's affair with the Countess.

At the end of one day, when the whole clan united in his offices one more time, Judge Gottschalk had them sign their testimonies. Then he announced that they were free to go for now. The actors were relieved if confused.

Marco wanted some more action for his money.

"What about the trial?"

Judge Gottschalk nodded with all seriousness.

"Oh yes, the trial. There certainly will be a murder trial. You can be sure of that."

Mail was already in the mailbox by the door. There was a letter from home; Leopold recognized Louisa's handwriting. Her governess taught her well. There was another one which he opened immediately.

His friend von Glaubitz had no news from the Innsbruck judiciary court, yet his friend remarked, "It might be safer to move from Weimar to your Burgenland estate."

Why did he say that? Did he have some unofficial information? He didn't write more about it. Instead. . .

"Soon," von Glaubitz continued without any further hint, "there will be steam-powered coaches on tracks connecting cities of Europe! That will be a different kind of travel, Poldi. You won't have to worry about getting a place in a postillion, nor to pay for your own carriages."

Leopold was irritated and didn't want to hear about progress.

Coaches on tracks? he thought, unable to buy into that idea. *We have to wait and see!*

He folded the letter and drank his second glass.

Quido is right. Burgenland is closer to Vienna. The family was expected to spend Christmas there this year. Also, Count had a letter from his estate, "This year's harvest promises great wines!"

"Done." Franz fixed the tie pin in Count's bright white knot of his tie. It was wrapped around his throat several times as the latest fashion dictated in Weimar. One of his last dinners there. He was meticulously dressed; his expensive clothes were an echo of the last Century_ the black Chinese brocade with all colors and motives of exotic birds; his powdered hair was another one of them.

The pin was new; his friend's present last Christmas. It was a lovely little thing—a golden needle topped with a small, golden lion's head with a deep red Bohemian garnet in his open mouth. His darling late wife's mother was of Bohemian nobility; Johann Wolfgang hasn't forgotten. She was their crush at one time when they were very young. The Count was touched.

He observed himself in the long, oval mirror standing by the opened French window, then began brushing his temples with tortoiseshell decorated brush. He waited until Franz tied his hair back with black silk ribbon. Then he leaned towards his image. His hair didn't turn more gray this past year—he was pleased to notice. His upper body was still pleasantly—if painfully—aware of his fencing practice yesterday. He felt hurting thighs and laughed off yet quite a different event. He felt energetic and for a moment thought that he should stay. But then reason won again.

Johann Wolfgang didn't approve of his altered plan. His speech was fluid and hard to interrupt.

"Home? Now? I thought you found it pleasant here, that we would have you through the next spring. What's the rush? Here you have it all! I actually thought you could move in here, perhaps even buy a house."

Leopold envied him yet couldn't quite imagine himself there in the mild landscape of large rivers, lakes, and gentle rolling hills.

Wolf looked at him and became slightly suspicious.

"I hope_ no bad news?"

Leopold glanced at his friend.

Bad news? What does he know?

His quick answer came soon enough to dissolve any doubts, "My estates need a man's hand at times like these." The unknown danger, his acute fear were not the only reasons.

He already craved his Alps; autumn hunt; trout in quick, icy-cold streams; waterfalls; short winter ski trips; and his beloved Burgenland of vineyard-covered hills running wild along lakes wherever you looked. It was suddenly clear to him that he absolutely must return home without any delay, fear or not.

Uncharacteristically, Wolfgang got drunk that night.

Burgenland!

Quido von Glaubitz decided to travel up here from his home in Innsbruck regardless of the looming war.

He missed Leopold, and he missed Burgenland in the autumn, with colorful vineyards and joyous wine festivals. This was his favorite place to be in the season of wine harvest.

As a journalist, he wasn't afraid of conflicts—he strived on them. So even if the predictions proved right, he would have been in the middle of action as an eyewitness for his readers.

Leopold stood up and opened his arms.

"I can't believe this! My friend! You are here!"

Their hug was the warm, uncomplicated, sincere gesture of true old friends. No words needed to express more.

Later, with both their meerschaums lit and running, Leopold carefully asked what was new in Innsbruck.

"Ah, I almost forgot! I have it here."

Von Glaubitz fished in the deep pocket of his coat and handed Leopold his paper, *The Blatt*.

"Looks like the actress talked after all. They say she will testify!"

Leopold glanced over the pages. His friend was excited.

"I am sorry I couldn't come sooner. The paper will fly off the printing press like town sparrows when you clap hands, now!"

Leopold sat there, his meek *Aha* couldn't satisfy his publisher friend. "C'mon Poldi! Say something isn't this sensational?!"

"Yes. Yes, of course it is absolutely sensational."

"Judges say it will be easy to bring the man to justice now. There's also someone else who remembers—a boy, her cousin."

"What cousin?"

"It says it here somewhere."

"Little Carlo," Leopold whispered, his voice dying down.

His friend didn't catch that as his eyes were running through the text.

"Here it is_ Carlo! He's about twenty. He will have something to say at the trial."

He handed the paper to Leopold and crossed to the large, cone shaped wooden urn.

"May I pour for you too, Poldi?""

"Yes! Please . . ."

Quido poured two full glasses of red.

Leopold woke up.

"A trial," he said as he took his wine and drank immediately.

His thoughts threatened to blow his skull open.

Could Carlo remember anything? He was a little child who could barely muster his Italian.

His friend observed him with growing concern. What was happening here?

"Well, not yet. They are gathering more testimonies and so on. It must be enormous paperwork, I bet. Twenty-some years!"

"So she testified."

"She'll be coming back to Innsbruck. There's a rumor going around that her father is not shy of blackmail or worse."

But Leopold stopped listening. Giovanna will be back then. She will describe him, and that will ruin him. He will lose it all_ his honor, his family name.

Before he gave his thoughts any further form, he heard himself saying, "Would you travel down to Milan with me if I asked you to?"

Von Glaubitz left his meerschaum in his mouth but moved it to the corner of his lips. It affected his speech in a particular way, which didn't come across as funny today.

"What about the possible war?"

"It's been around for years, it never stopped us."

This was true, Quido knew that. They would travel together at times like these.

"Would you come?" Count repeated.

There was a fine layer of nostalgia in Quido's answer, "That's the kind of trip we used to always enjoy—no preparations, quickly out! Oh, those times."

But Quido of today was a rational man.

"Those times are long gone. No thank you, my friend. I'll pass."

He took a sip.

"Nice wine you have here."

Leopold lifted his glass and examined the color.

"That was an exceptional year, 1801. They tell me that this year will be as good, if not better."

"This peace is not going to last," Quido noted as he dipped the sugary *Burgenländer kipferl* in his wine.

Leopold heard the coach stopping, the clicking of horseshoes. Voices of footmen. He took off his pince-nez. *Quido returned to go to Milan!*

The carriage-door was opened. There was the familiar sound of the three steps unfolding with a loud crack. Then he recognized his daughter-in-law's voice.

"All my luggage up to my room!" The Countess commanded her valets and maids.

Her steps were uncharacteristically loud, reminding him of Frederik's.

She started talking the moment she stood in the door—no *hello*, no curtsies, no stretched arms, no hugs. She rushed here from Innsbruck with one goal.

"I beg you," she said unceremoniously.

With her traveling clothes still on, she sounded more urgent than ever. The letter she dispatched only a few days ago said briefly without any further explanation, "I'm coming. Wait for me, please."

Leopold guessed instantly that Quido visited her after his return. He understood.

She only took down her veiled hat. Her voice changed and came in her usual soft manner, "Please teach him . . . sometime soon."

Her eyes, the color of dark violets, started brimming with tears; she was looking at her father-in-law's broad back dressed in fine Chinese brocade. It was woven in gold and silk—joyful, bright colors like a playful children's painting. It failed to make her smile.

She rushed to get there before everybody. She was exhausted. Perhaps she should wait. It wasn't easy to put more urgency in her voice. Yet, she tried.

"He's your heir . . ." It was barely audible as she dreaded it would.

Leopold von Schönbruck, her father-in-law, was standing there absolutely unnerved. But she didn't sense it. As if all her instincts left her except for one: maternal.

He feared that resolve. He was not certain what to say next. She wasn't sure anymore that he knew she was there.

"Father?"

Count's arms habitually folded on his chest.

He heard her well. His was the difficult decision which he'd been postponing successfully for years.

She needed his answer, his reassurance, "I am his mother, I beg you."

Count von Schönbruck had predicted this confrontation—his opinions were organized with exactness of a general he hadn't aspired to be.

Finally, he turned towards her. His right hand rested on the side table where his mineral and fossil collection was placed; his left hand formed a tight fist and was pressed to his waistline despite sharp pain; folds of his fine silk shirt obscured his mutilated fingers. His voice was no more calm.

"I am not sure about him," Count said. "You see, I can't teach him the secret maneuver unless I know for certain."

He hoped she wouldn't press that issue; the secret maneuver had failed her husband—mysteriously, but it did. Yet, there she was, pushing him to teach it to her eldest son!

Her voice was holding her emotions back, tightening her throat.

"Please, give him that secret, teach it to him. He is entitled."

"Entitled?"

Count pushed from the table. His collections dangerously shook, but the piece of furniture didn't topple.

She recognized too late that her word was not well chosen.

"Nobody here is entitled to anything until I say so. No. I'm sorry, Madame. Absolutely not."

His patience was spent; he wanted all this to be over, quickly and forever. His opinion was clear. Now he saw it with relief, "The sooner he's off to the army . . ."

He intended to say the better, but all of a sudden, he wasn't certain about that. His hesitation gave her the rare moment. She didn't wait, "But that's it!"

Her shout surprised them both. She stood up and faced him for the first time ever. She didn't beg for his pardon, as usual either. She plunged into her plea on top of her voice,

"Army! Battles! Duels! All of that bloody nonsense! You have the best weapon to protect him! Then give it to him!"

"It's not the best, you know it as well as I do! It failed!" he shouted back at her.

She wasn't listening any longer. Her voice was flying forward, hurting his face.

"What if not? Teach him! Fred must have something to protect himself with! Can't you see? You must! You must do it for him!"

That was the moment to slam his face with her deepest secret, to shout out loud the whole truth about his darling son, about his duel, his whore—to blackmail him with those horrid facts! His mind tried to grasp her words.

What did she mean by 'What if not'?

Marie-Antonia took a deep breath. Her voice turned dark as she unexpectedly slowed down her lament.

"I know, I know all about my husband's death I . . ."

She got his attention now.

"What do you know?" was more of a deep sound than a question, he couldn't recognise his own voice.

Leopold's face turned pale, his eyes transfixed on hers. He observed her the way a lion eyes his prey, waiting for a false move to end this scene.

She found herself in a dangerous, strange, unknown territory. His voice was dark, his eyes sharp like green blades of grass.

A memory fleshed through her inner eye; just a few seconds.

It was that actress from the Burgtheater . . . what was her name now? Desiree or something? Her soliloquy made such an impression—Queen Clytemnestra trying to save her child Iphigenia from her own father, playing va banque because there was nothing to lose . . .

"What is it you know?"

Marie-Antonia didn't possess the fierceness of the ancient Greek heroine, but she suddenly saw that she had everything to lose. If she tells him, it will destroy him; it will destroy them all. He is her only family, her children's only relative, her protector.

"I am a woman." A safe benign remark didn't make him suspicious. He was too exhausted for that. It simply angered him, "You know nothing."

The male voice was a stranger—unkind, unwilling to listen any further. The Count turned away.

She didn't dare to say more. Her quivering fingers rearranged some of the flowers in the vase on the side table. She slowly merged into the cushions of a settee. One by one she started guiding her fingers out of her long, white kidskin gloves.

Leopold's thoughts were already far away. A view of a young man—him himself—standing over a dead body, his sword covered in blood. He interrupted that thought by quick steps towards the door.

Before leaving the room, he said over his shoulder, "I can't."

At the door, he turned and faced her again. He pronounced his words as if she were deaf.

"I will never give our secret to anyone, as long as I shall live."

ACT V

It was some move from the Alps to the Burgenland! Thank goodness they do it only every third year.

Louisa, her little siblings, nannies, governesses, Frau Ebner, Thomas, and everybody else arrived positively broken after a long trip.

The Burgenland chateau was Leopold's family's estate. It was a safe haven for him always. There was no memento reminding him of his tragic loss that he could have come across.

Louisa, still waking up in the carriage, thought that she didn't hear correctly.

"Frederik and Tristan will be in Vienna for months?"

She couldn't believe it. Her beloved grandpapa came home from Weimar, but her brother didn't wait for her. The family was in pieces again. She felt like crying.

Lucky that Mama was still here before going to join those two in Vienna.

This year was one of those when the whole household would move there for autumn festivals, Christmas, and Easter. Then they would stay until roads dried out and return home to Innsbruck.

The Countess wanted Louisa's first ball to be here. She was certain that her father-in-law wouldn't object to that.

When the coaches arrived, Leopold heard the hustle-bustle in the courtyard and had no intention to go out. He stayed at the library, but it took only minutes for his young grandsons to find him.

Their little sister, Sophie, climbed on his lap and, with the most endearing gesture, took Leopold's cheeks in her little palms. She looked deeply in his eyes from such a short distance that he thought he would go cross-eyed. With loving simplicity, she discovered him again.

"There is my Opa!"

They all made more noise, were fetched by nannies, and taken to their rooms with promises they would see him at dinner, all in a quick sequence which, Leopold had already forgotten, was an inevitable part of their days.

Then there was the sound of satin slippers and a female voice said, "Opapa."

Count stood up. His heart couldn't find its proper place for a moment. When it did, he felt that the sound must have shaken the whole estate.

"Louisa?"

Her likeness with his late wife, Louisa, took his breath away.

No more short hair but natural light brown curls parted in the middle and long tresses tamed by a pale blue satin ribbon and pinned up high. She was the copy of her grandmother she never knew. Here was the image from portraits Count had burnt in a weak attempt to escape pain and heartache.

She stood in front of him—his Louisa, his only love, reborn, coming afresh to his life.

Leopold knew immediately that there's no will in him to fight that battle one more time.

Louisa rushed forward, curtsied to him, and kissed first his hand and then his cheeks. He was mute, afraid he might scare this image away.

"Opa? What is the matter?"

Leopold was not capable of forming any thoughts. There were no words he would dare to say to her at this moment. Louisa stood there until the rustle of heavy silk made her turn.

"Mama!"

"Here you are! At last!" Marie-Antonia, Countess von Schönbruck, saved the awkward moment. She walked in, her arms stretched to welcome her daughter. Louisa rushed towards her ending in a slight curtsy.

"Oh, Mama! How was your trip?"

Their conversation was muffled by voices of all other children quickly coming and running, talking one over the other. Leopold was saved. His strong voice found his grandchildren.

"My dears! How I had missed you! It seems like ages since the last time we were together!"

Count was watching them with awe. His love for them all was balm for his heart aches. He couldn't allow anybody and anything to destroy it.

This was a new picture of his little family. He noticed the renewed, relaxed, amiable manner of them all.

They surrounded their mother, flooding her with news and observations from their trip. It was so much easier to be with her ever since she took those dark habits off and started wearing bright colors!

There they were! He watched them through the most perplexing yet the happiest moment of his life. He stopped fighting his affection.

"Wouldn't you say that Louisa's ready for her first ball?"

The Countess turned to her father-in-law. She carefully watched his face. There was not a shadow left from their difficult conversation. She saw his face turning softer, his eyes changing hues and shining the way she's never seen in him.

Only now Leopold felt safe to go back to his granddaughter and embrace her.

"My dear, look at you! You are a young lady now! I would tip my hat to you, had I met you on the street! Never could I have guessed this is my little girl Louisa!"

They all laughed a happy, sincere laughter; theirs were the easy agreements of a family together again— an effortless accord after being separated for a long period of time.

Count opened his arms, and all the little ones crowded the wide space on his chest.

"Grandpapa!" the little ones squealed.

Leopold held them warmly, his mind already elsewhere.

Out of blue he remembered a lovely little thing—a sweet surprise long expired. He'd never had a chance to give it to his bride. It just presented an unexpected possibility. He became excited and forgot all about danger and fear.

The Countess had written left and right, dispatching a tall stack of letters to friends, neighbors, dance masters, dressmakers, shoemakers, pastry chefs in Vienna. The ball was announced. An orchestra of Viennese musicians was hired and a dance master selected.

Officers staying during ongoing army exercises in the nearby small town were summoned up. Social dances of the day were part of their training. In those times, balls and dancing parties had always been the highlight of military life. This one was promising.

A letter came from Fredrik with regrets. He'll be unable to get away from the academy. In earlier days, Louisa would have been sorely disappointed; but on that very day, she received the most unexpected present from her grandpapa—the loveliest dance book in mother-of-pearl covers with her miniature portrait on the top!

How did he manage that?

Leopold felt his palms sweating.

I wish you'll write down my name for every dance, he hoped but couldn't tell if he just said that out loud.

His cheeks turned crimson. His granddaughter's smiling eyes were reassuring. She saw him with surprising freshness. She kept her observations tactfully to herself. *Is Opa blushing?*

Leopold was trapped. Louisa kissed his cheek, curtseyed, and went upstairs to get dressed.

Tonight Louisa was being dressed by two maids. First balls were a very special occasion. Mother even lent her two of her turquoise hair combs. Around her tight chignon, Louisa tucked fresh, fragrant pink roses. When she dressed in a long, pale blue dress—gathered in the back to open wide during dancing, floating with every movement—she felt very adult. Her fine silk scarf was her grandfather's gift.

She was almost out the door when Mama called her back" I almost forgot…"

"Here."

The Countess handed her oldest daughter a new silk fan. It had sides made of intricately cut ivory, looking like lace. This was the briseé fan, the latest scream of fashion.

"Mama, oh, how exquisite! Thank you! How did you know I wished for it?"

The Secret Maneuver

Louisa couldn't stop smiling; she stepped towards her mother and kissed her hand. Her mother put her arms around her.

"My little girl no more. Have fun tonight, darling!" Marie-Antonia kissed her cheeks. "I will see you at the ball. Now I must have my hair finished." Louisa curtseyed and went downstairs to the parlor to wait for the coach. She felt like dancing already.

Her grandfather was there and stood up as she entered. That was a first. It took them both by surprise. The room filled up with soft, agreeable silence.

Count Leopold and his granddaughter, the young Countess Louisa, stood there facing each other—just looking, beaming.

"You look very beautiful, my dear—very adult, if I may say so."

"Thank you. Yes you may, my . . . my Opa."

She finally stepped forward and, just like when she was a little girl, hugged him with the full length of her petite body, putting her head on his perfectly pressed jacket and remained there.

Leopold closed his arms around her fragile shoulders, bent down and his lips found silk of her hair; they stayed in the company of fragrant flowers. Afraid to breath, they remained in absolute silence, until someone said in the hallway, "My lord, your coach is ready."

Magic stayed in the room behind them. They didn't look at each other. Down in the courtyard, two lines of servants with flickering torches lit their passage. They walked through the espalier of warm light towards the dark void of their carriage.

Louisa side glanced Count's face; she couldn't recognize the young man walking next to her. They traveled the short distance without words; it wasn't the heavy, oppressing burden of vacuum but silence filled with joy, all-embracing happiness, and love.

When he thought of these moments hours later, he questioned his feelings. Was it his imagination? Did she stay in his arms because—or only *because*—he is her grandfather, out of respect? Because that's what grandfathers do? He was afraid to answer them.

This was madness; he must go away or he will destroy what he should cherish and observe with joy from a distance. Leopold was in love, the way he'd forgotten existed.

In the perplexing parallel, he discovered the shocking truth about getting old—forever there remains the young person inside the human mind and body. The body is sent its own way to deteriorate, to malfunction, to wrinkle, to crack, to fall apart. And yet in his feelings, his desire, his senses, he was surely no more than twenty.

His palms burnt as much as they used to when he touched the fingertips of his wife-to-be, Louisa. His mind was in a haze, he felt like staying in bed all day long, feeling ill as if a cold was preparing to attack. He loved again! Leopold decided to face his challenge, and stay.

The ballroom was a vast, tall, airy space, with one side full of French windows. Seven large, gilded, five-tier Bohemian crystal chandeliers were lit with hundreds of candles. Their yellow, bright flames flickered in the reflection on the opposite wall, completely covered in mirrors in gilded rococo frames. The effect doubled the brightness and multiplied the enthusiastic crowd.

Louisa was introduced left, right, turned, was ushered to an old duchess, to meet Mama's friends from Vienna then back and then—

"Frederik!"

Her brother was standing there in his most glamorous hussar uniform. He seemed taller, grew a thin mustache, and his many long braids were perfectly tight and glossy, silver wire in their ends. He turned towards his mother,

"Countess, how enchanting you look tonight!" She let him kiss her hand, and he bowed.

They taught him manners in the academy! she observed to herself with a very public proud smile.

He then switched his attention to his sister,

"And you, young Countess, you look divine tonight!"

Louisa burst out laughing.

"How did you manage? I am so happy you've come!"

"The first dance is mine!"

"I don't know, I must look." Her air of a young lady took Frederik by surprise. He felt his impatience building up. Louisa opened her little booklet. "No, sorry. The next dance I will dance with—"

"With me!"

Frederik lifted her and started spinning with her. Louisa's dance slipper flew away. Some shocked ladies exclaimed, but everything turned into a joke the moment his grandfather, the Count, crossed the room.

He picked up Louisa's dance slipper and felt the eyes of the whole ballroom on him. He walked up to his grandchildren,

"And who is this young man here? Frederik, what a magnificent uniform! Let me look at you!"

He hesitated with the slipper in his hand. He wished there was no one in the room so he could kneel down and put it on Louisa's slender foot.

"Oh, Opa! Thank you!"

Louisa took her slipper from his hand and, taking Frederik's forearm as her support, slid the dark red-silk-satin masterpiece on.

Frederik tucked her arm under his and said, "Grandpapa! You still dance?"

"More than ever! How's Vienna these days?"

The music started with an introduction. The dance master called another dance, and the young officer, whose name Louisa wrote down an hour ago, came for his dance.

Frederik stepped in front of his sister.

"The Countess, my sister, will not dance this turn."

The young officer clicked his heels, gave a short brisk nod, and went back to sit with his friends.

Louisa wanted to be angry. She looked at Fred, but he made one of his funny faces, which made her giggle every time. Her anger was gone. Frederik was happy.

"It works! It still works! You are still my little Louisa," Frederik smiled broadly at his eldest sister. He took her hand and led her forward. Their hands felt the old familiar rush. Only this was no longer the safety of their Alpine valley.

The Count watched the scene from a short distance. Frederik and Louisa.

He didn't know what to do. He was jealous.

It was consuming his judgement. The only way to survive this, without making an old fool of himself, was to _walk away.

The cool breeze on the terrace didn't bring him any relief. He took several deep breaths. He thought he was there only for a minute and was looking for a drink when quick light steps approached him.

"Grandpapa!" Louisa said behind him. "The 'Mr. Beveridge's Maggot' is next. I hoped you would dance it with me."

He wanted to say "I cannot" and to turn and leave the ball. But her hand was already clutching his, and they stepped back into the ballroom as the music already played the intro for that sweet dance.

The swaying, fleeting touches of hands and shoulders, the sudden waves towards each other and away, the longing of hands, the slow spinning around each other, the promenade of bodies as if this were a metaphor of Leopold's love—he tried to focus on his steps. But there was *his* Louisa, the day they got married and danced "Maggot" as their first dance as husband and wife.

When they stopped, Louisa stayed down in her deep curtsy longer than the dancers around her.

She had to recover her feelings. Green pools of her grandfather's eyes rushing against her with_ *it was longing? Wasn't it?*

Her head bent down, she remained until Frederik lifted her arm. She gave a start and stood up. Her brother planted a kiss on her hand.

"I confess, you are a Princess! You danced divinely!"

Leopold stood there watching his daughter-in-law taking Louisa's shoulder and navigating her towards a young man in a dragoon uniform, standing with his parents at the end of the room. He was one of the most sought-after bachelors of Viennese high aristocracy.

When later the quadrille came on the program, Louisa, Frederik, and the dragoon with his cousin were put together. Louisa noticed that the young lady had eyes only for Frederik. He seemed to enjoy it immensely and forgot to be jealous of the dragoon!

With another dance, Frederik was elsewhere, and Louisa had some freedom. The young dragoon came for her again, prompted by her mother. Louisa couldn't believe how smoothly he danced. She had never felt like she was flying. The waltz was the new dance that everybody had been practicing—he danced it divinely! She was floating in the air. They danced three more times together. He was smitten. She wasn't sure what she felt.

He liked that Louisa was careful not to reveal much; it was clear to him that she liked him a great deal. Her mother was adamant that he visits them soon.

The ball was a huge success. Several matches were made. Ladies showed off their new fashions from Viennese salons, and some, secretly, from La Parisienne fashion leaves. To hell with Napoleon if there's a ball to go to!

Next week, the young nobleman called on Louisa and her family. The Countess started planning Louisa's future. Count was standing there, watching. When he was asked, he gave his opinion.

"I thought you liked him," said his daughter-in-law, puzzled, "Why not? His family has a high standing in Vienna. Their family tree is as long as ours. What do you mean by 'he's inadequate'?"

No, this is not right. It feels so odd, so improper__ so good! Desiree caught herself thinking about the last few weeks as the planker was taking her across the muddy Viennese side street by the Burgtheater.

She was standing on the wheeled wooden plank, holding his shoulder. Her black waxed-cotton galoshes were tied on the side of her slim ankles with red ribbons. She held her dress in a pinch, paying little attention to the wind. Little applause flew towards her as her thighs flashed for a second to delight some dandies standing in front of the cigar store up the street. She smiled under the white brim of her chapeau but didn't turn her head.

Her shoulders were wrapped in a cozy long, white fox boa—her wealthy lover's parting gift. She already had a new male face on her mind, not without doubts for sure. The boy was too young; she had never had a man younger than herself but, and she had a point there, he comes every night with large bouquets of flowers. At her age, it started happening less and less. So what. He's wealthy and devoted. *He is also very romantic, he is smitten and in love, he says. It is a little odd maybe. But I'm an actress and I am bored.*

His companion is older though. And as rich as the boy, it seems and handsome he is, our eyes locked the second we were introduced. He really is much brighter than the junior. He seems to be well versed in literature and theatre.

She paused, suddenly disturbed by an emotion she didn't want here, to complicate this adventure, to make it feel like the real thing she'd been waiting for but gave up years ago.

Let's see! I like new adventures, and this one could be a twosome in the end.

The thing was thrilling even further—the younger man resembled her first love, Georg.

Come to think of it, she had another lover once—briefly—who looked so much like him as well. *Do I always pick the same man?* Her hand with a golden ring covered her wide full mouth as she gave a loud laugh. The swallows on it didn't stop chasing each other.

She must be imagining now that he was obsessed with her. He was an officer. She gave him one of her embroidered kerchiefs with the cipher *G*. Yes, she can admit it now; she loved him madly too. Briefly. He folded the fine kerchief and carried it on his heart. He was the only one who knew that Desiree was her stage name.

He ended up badly, she'd heard. He was a hussar. A girl must not fall for a soldier of any kind. She knew that now. He was one of the most exciting men. She knew his full name__Carl-Maria von Schönbruck. She will never forget him.

The planker stopped. She paid him the second half of his asking price. This one was a nice man, not like the grouch on the other side of the theatre. The young man offered his arm, and she safely pushed from the plank.

"Goodbye, beauty!" the planker exclaimed.

With a large spring step, she crossed the space left and landed on the sidewalk free of all doubts. Her laughter and a flash of her upper thigh were as good as a tip for him.

She started rushing towards the stage door. Exuberant, full of energy and high spirits she entered the theatre.

All was clear. A new, exciting era had opened up for her—Tristan and Fred!

The narrow alley was still dark in the early hours of the day. Dr. Horace Kilner stopped to relieve himself. He hoped to get to bed for a few moments before the day gets going. Birds in the Old Vienna were already chirping.

That was a long night! Much longer than he'd anticipated.

It started with the difficult breech birth at the house of his friend, the imperial judge, during which he was called out to the inn. He had to stitch up two miserable bums who did not know any better than to fight with broken glasses over a prostitute.

He delivered a healthy boy. The judge was generous with his pay—after two girls, a boy! He was home for the birth from Innsbruck. He had a murder case there, an old murder. Their little girls were such a screaming nuisance. Her nanny, what did they call her? Anneliese! She had a wandering eye for sure. Pretty little thing.

The doctor was finally heading home—tired, buzzed from two jugs of the lager he drank too quickly in a small pub just round the corner from the hospital.

As he turned towards the wall, he saw a bunch of old rags on the ground and kicked them away while unbuttoning his pants. The rags screamed and showered him with drunken swear words from the gutter they camped in.

Horace was startled and peed over the front of his trousers. Among dried alcohol spills, it was just one more territory on the dark blue map of his suit. He came home and crashed without undressing.

They woke him up around noon; he had barely a moment to wash his face! He was trying to keep up with the police messenger.

"Hurry, hurry there's been a murder!" The messenger was pulling on his elbow.

Horace couldn't hurry—he was still half asleep!

The theatre outer staircase was on the side that led to the hay market. On the opposite side, it bordered the old building of the university.

During the day, the whole area was the noisiest crossroad of human lives and emotions. They were played out loudly without scruples in the opened market; shouts exchanged during bargaining around the small vendors' colorful stands.

An occasional scream of a woman who got pinched by someone's wandering hand, a slap of a quick hand fishing for a ladies' reticule, followed by strings of swear words were nothing strange—just like a man, simply dressed, who was rushing down the street, avoiding carts and horses, with his jacket splashed with some paint or something.

That morning, Marius, the theatre janitor, was limping through the backstage corridor carrying the second of twelve buckets of water. They had to be placed around the stage in case of fire.

He used to be this theatre's biggest star once. He was second only to the Divine Vigano! Like him, his jumps and turns left audiences gasping. He knew how to dance, he knew how to act, and when he killed himself in Romeo and Juliet, ladies in the audience used to faint. He was to become the Divine Marius!

The metal pail he was dragging hit the wooden floor. Water splashed on the ground.

Marius cursed under his alcohol-saturated breath and looked for a rag or a shawl left behind somewhere to wipe this. But no such luck today. He had to limp all the way back, the sharp pain shooting from his damaged hip all through his upper body.

He stopped and reached inside his worn-down costume jacket. The silver clasps were long gone—traded them all for a drink.

The typical flat clear-glass flask was still half full of homemade slivovitz. He smiled and took another long swig. His next step became more of sway as he grasped the backdrop curtain to stop himself from falling. But either he was too heavy or the fabric too old; he ripped it and fell through. Anger ignited all his old unsolved defeats. He was scrambling through the drapes; his swearing litany came out loud and getting louder. He scrambled through the ripped scenery back.

He couldn't have been that drunk for when he looked on the floor, he saw many more drops. Dark spots all over. He limped back to wipe some, tossed the rag back in the water, lifted it again, wrenched it, and started sobering up.

The water gradually changed color; it went from yellow to brown to pink. He stared at the veils of red dye slowly turning inside the water. He was trying to remember where he saw it the last time. Then it hit him. This was not some paint from a repaired backdrop. This was blood.

"Anybody there?"

Sudden fear got a grip of his voice chords. He slowly turned, looked around, afraid to move now, and waited. There was silence smudged by the muffled noise of the nearby square market. He walked back to the place where he saw the first drops.

At the corridors' crossing he took down the lit oil lantern from the wall. He held it up to light up the path in front of him as the dark dots lead into the corridor. There were more and more of them.

He called again, "Anybody there!"

This time his voice sounded a bit stronger. The door in front of him was ajar. Odd since the dressing room of stars remained always closed. He walked slowly forward.

Drops of blood were all over the floor now, some smudged, more of them closer together. Then he saw it—a puddle of blood. It had already saturated the wooden floor, soaked the small round carpet laying in front of a pink velvet divan, and started drying out around its edge. The dressing screen stood across. Marius felt queasy.

A few moments later, his hand clutched the brass handles and shook the window. But the window frame was stuck! He had to fight it, but when he decided to break the glass, it opened out.

"Help! Help! Murder!"

His voice was trembling, weakened by the effort, by alcohol, by fear.

An uneven cadence of his chant fought its way out into the loud cacophony of the street noise. His throat turned hoarse and sore. Then finally, after chanting "murder" for what felt like eternity, he saw a gendarme running up the street from his regular post across the theatre.

Marius called to him and waved, "Come! Come! Murder! Here! Hurry! Come!"

He stood there waiting by the window. His legs were shaking. He kept repeating his call, "Help! Murder!" When he saw the gendarme finally running towards the entrance, he added, "They murdered Desiree!"

Dr. Kilner's pants stayed unbuttoned until the police inspector pointed that out to him.

"Your pants, doctor." Then, without the slightest undertone, revealing any sort of judgement, he asked,

"Do you know this woman?"

"Of course I know this woman! Everybody knows this woman." Doctor, irritated, visibly surprised, barked back while fixing his pants. He looked around and then, with slight hesitation, turned back at the police official.

"You don't?"

"Suicide?" asked the inspector, disregarding the doctor's tone.

Doctor hesitated.

"She wouldn't have walked out there then come here. I will need more time to look at her."

Commissar's experienced eyes were examining the unfamiliar surroundings.

So this is what backstage looks like, he thought, giving a quick nod.

"Right. Now tell me, doctor, who is she?"

The theatre seemed to be empty now, long hours before actors gathered for tonight's performance. Dressers—the little women always first to be present to do all of the mending, ironing, embellishing—appeared magically from nowhere. Their usual cheerfulness was cut short right at the door by a policeman.

"Somebody should wait at the door and tell him," suggested one of the dressers hauling costumes down the spiral staircase.

The chief inspector who just arrived turned his head and looked at his inspector.

"Tell who?"

But his tired man had no answer and only turned crimson red.

"Her fiancée," finished the dresser, a younger woman, skinny and barely visible in the petticoats she carried above her head now.

"Desiree's fiancé?"

"Desiree? I didn't know she had one." Dr. Kilner was honestly surprised.

"Anything about him? Any information? His name, perhaps? Who is he? Description?" The chief inspector was not armed with patience. He stared down the commissar. All he saw was a panicked, blank look. He turned his eyes toward the ceiling. *Who are these people I'd employed? On whose recommendations was this one here hired?*

"He will be here tonight, all right," said possibly the youngest of the dressers as she looked at her older counterparts. But they didn't have anything to add.

"He comes every day, you know. With the largest bouquet . . . I mean . . . huge. I mean over the top," continued the dresser.

Nobody giggled today as this was not like any other day when they could gossip about Desiree.

Yet it encouraged a petite blonde, plump and cross-eyed. "He's not what you'd call handsome. His eyes are so far apart, he's a little odd.

The first one decided to chime in, "Strange but rich!"

They suppressed giggles, but some of the others seemed to disagree.

"He's not strange. He's just young and in love, oh so enamored."

Now they talked one over another. It was more to make noise than to help, more to show they were the insiders there and to fight their fear.

"The name! His name?"

They seemed not to hear the inspector, but then a dresser's help came in, her arms full of repaired skirts and said,

"Tristan, his name is Tristan."

"Did she have any enemies?" the chief inspector asked as he followed the theatre director to his office.

"Desiree?" the theatre director answered without any enthusiasm. "The whole town is divided between her lovers and those she turned down. There. Speaking of her enemies..."

The chief inspector didn't like the arrogant man from the moment he stepped across this theatre threshold.

"What can you tell me about your whereabouts between midnight and noon? And what about your relationship with Miss Desiree?"

"We were young once."

"Lovers?"

"Hers or mine?"

"Don't be clever with me. Did you owe her money?"

That did it. With a raised voice, the director leaned towards the inspector's face.

"I beg your pardon? I have been many things, but no one ever called me a miser! She's been paid like a queen!"

"She surely brings—*brought*—great business to your establishment."

"This is a theatre with tradition, sir. Serious stuff, long-standing classics! Such you've probably never even heard of!"

The chief inspector turned deaf ear to this unkind tirade and repeated his question.

The director took a deep breath.

"As far as last night, I played Kaiserspiel 'till three at my house, then had a girl with me 'til we left together to come here now. You can talk to her if you wish."

Annella was eighteen, eager to become a star.

"All he said is true," she said. "I sat with him, I am his... lucky charm."

She smiled back at the director, but he wasn't looking at her.

"Then we went to bed," she sighed, saying it without any shame, fear, or single thought of being judged.

The side stage door, which nobody from the police had noticed before, opened abruptly.

A very young man walked in with an older companion in tow. The ridiculously huge bouquet of flowers identified him immediately.

The chief inspector, a father of three teenage boys himself, just could not make himself believe that he's looking at Desiree's lover.

Desiree was probably in her early forties; her colorful life could not be hidden by any makeup much longer. It was the quality of her extraordinary voice, her emotional scale, and her impeccable comical timing that was still keeping her in the rank of the stars. She kept being desired by men of all ages and social standing. Desiree—desire personified.

The chief inspector stepped towards the young man carrying bouquets.

"Tristan?"

"Good evening!" The superiority of that tone, the heavy gold signet ring which bore his coat of arms, his golden tie pin—all was carefully put on display if anybody would have had any doubt who was standing in front of them.

God help me, this is Frederik von Schönbruck! The doctor realized with relief that the young man didn't recognize him in this poor light.

It was barely a month ago when the doctor was called to assist after a duel—a lucky one, at that. Nobody got killed, just scratches. He treated Frederik. They were young officers from the military academy, not well trained yet_lucky.

The chief inspector saw the doctor's face and was surprised to see his shocked reaction.

"And you are?" the young man turned towards the official.

"I am Chief Inspector Weinbach of the Imperial Police." he said capitalizing his titles, "I'm here to investigate a murder."

The young man did not even look at him and pushed around.

"I have more pleasant business here, gentlemen."

He gave them a brisk nod and started walking away towards Desiree's dressing room.

Desiree's dressing lady was the quickest of them all. She stepped in front of the young gentleman, almost tumbling his older friend down.

"You can't, young sir! You cannot, tonight, I am so sorry . . ."

He shoved her aside and started running forward.

"Des?"

They all rushed after him.

The effect it had on the young man was something the chief inspector would never forget.

The bouquet dropped from the young man's arms as he shot forward.

Before anyone could stop him, he rushed through. His companion, pale and stumbling behind, was left at the door.

Desiree's dead body was placed on the pink velvet sofa by now, covered with a large square scarf. The young man pulled off the shawl, and covering the dead actress with kisses, he held her in his arms, his sobs filled up the theatre backstage. Then he suddenly turned towards the whole room. His hands started pulling down her costumes, colorful gowns, tearing down curtains, hitting the walls, smashing the looking glass with one of the porcelain jars holding her rouge, tearing the scarves that were arranged around the mirror frame.

"My Des! My love!" he shouted. "I am so sorry . . . forgive me. Come back! Don't leave me! Love me again! Oh, please, forgive me! Everything . . . I'm punished . . . punished, Des! My Des, De-si-ree!"

The doctor caught the exhausted young body in time before it could hit the floor. Together with the young man's companion, they carried the limp body to the director's office.

The doctor opened his bag and tried the sniffing salts.

"This should help."

Although a strong drink, in his opinion, might have had a much better effect.

"Poor boy. Take him home."

He turned to the companion, but the other young man stood there pale, lifeless, as if it was he who was just killed.

"Come, come. You need a drink here." The director poured him a full glass of schnapps. He had to help the young man to drink.

"You can't collapse just yet. Your young friend needs you. He just lost his love."

The chief inspector made up his mind. The two young men can leave. Nothing in here the young nobleman had to deal with. A carriage was brought to the front for the two young gentlemen.

"If you need me, Inspector, I'll be in the men's dressing room."

The theatre director turned and walked across the empty stage. Without scenery, its tall, dark brick sides looked disturbingly like a tomb.

Desiree was dead. Tristan's eyes stayed open, his face expressionless. It made no difference where or if they were riding to Frederik's home.

His sweet lover—the woman of his dreams—murdered in such a brutal, mad, unthinkable way! Stabbed many times over by a madman. Tristan's temples were pounding. He had a headache. He wished for something strong to drink, to drink until he was dead. He tried not to reveal any of that to Fredrik, not to upset him, not to raise suspicion. Even if it seemed all redundant now. The woman they both loved was gone. Whatever had led to this day had vanished into history.

They finally stopped at an inn to get fresh water and oats for their horses.

Frederik jumped down from his saddle and said unexpectedly, "Some women are really stupid." Then he noticed the building in front of them, "Which inn is this?"

Before anybody from the people sitting outside could answer, he saw the name.

"I know this one. Grandfather stays here when he travels. We'll stay the night. The estate is only half a day from here."

Tristan didn't question anything anymore—ever since he agreed to switch their names for their ventures in the Viennese theatre world, he felt he had no right.

Frederik pressed his face into Tristan's sleeve.

"I love you so much!" Then he looked at his tutor with dark intensity. "You are my only friend now. You'll love me forever, right?"

There was no safe space for any other answer but "Yes of course, Frederik. Yes, forever."

Frederik's strong arms hugged Tristan's; it felt more like an iron cuff than a friendship. Tristan had no energy in the midst of his headache to think about what just happened.

They handed their horses to the stable boy and entered the inn.

"We're staying tonight. You have two rooms?"

The innkeeper was glad. Travelers started being more and more rare. Times had become uncertain all over Europe again. There was much talk about Napoleon's new plans.

The two young men sat down on the corner bench by the small, low window full of geraniums.

"Schnapps!" ordered Tristan.

"Champagne!" called Frederik.

Their drinks in hand, they drank to life. The strong, peppery, bittersweet scent of geraniums and salvia successfully blocked the world out there.

The evening turned out warm and balmy. Autumn skies were colored in shades of reds and orange—the heralds of a windy day.

Tristan couldn't sleep. He drank too much, but it didn't help. The reason was too great to reconcile. The past weeks had become a nightmare.

Ever since his eye caught Desiree's, their fate was sealed. They started working their way towards each other—carefully at first, as every first heartbeat of love is a doubled solo without any other voices. Once the main theme orchestrates the full mass of emotions, there's no way to recreate the small chamber setting.

They were certain that nobody knew. To think that a young man of slow wits would be clever enough to understand, was beyond possible. They had taken off their guard. When they couldn't be together, they would write; they would burn the letters immediately after reading them, memorizing them. They would quote from Shakespeare, Schiller—Tristan could still remember passages from some of them.

Piecing the last weeks together now, he had to admit that maybe they were wrong; their love's blind assumption that they were discreet was madness. He could see it now.

Servants—they must have noticed, Tristan wondered.

There was one letter he couldn't recall burning. He looked for it everywhere—to no avail.

Did a servant sell it to Desiree's jealous former lover?

Fear, in its dark, blurred silhouette, started receiving sharper contours.

Tristan was tossing on the narrow bed—hay-stuffed mattress, bulky and hard was of no help.

Brief dreams kept trading places with visions, fragments of talks, images pulled out of context__

__The day Desiree was found—early morning, at dawn—Fred pushed open the door to Tristan's bedroom.

"Wake up!"

"Fred, you are smudged with blood?"

"A duel. We must leave. I dueled, and I hurt the man."

"You killed the man?"

"No, no! Just hurt him."

"To the first blood?"

"Yes, first blood"

"Who knows about it?"

"No one."

"Then you don't have to worry. The other man won't tell."

Frederik slowed down his movements. That's right. Nobody knows about his movements in the early morning. He was safe. He sat down heavily on a chair and issued a command,

"Give me some water."

The tutor in Tristan wanted to say "please," to prompt his student; but since Fred entered the daily training at the military academy, things between them had changed.

Tristan poured a glass full of water and brought it to Fred.

"Here."

There was no thank-you either. Count von Schönbruck wouldn't be amused.

Tristan had something pressing to take care of—something that was on his consciousness for some time now. He wished to make it right forever, to come out clean. He wanted to tell Desiree his real name as soon as possible.

"How about our theatre plans for tonight?" Tristan said, turning to Frederik.

There was silence. Frederik walked back into his room, poured water into his porcelain washbasin, and looked around for a towel.

He took off his boots, took off his blood-stained shirt, and unbuttoned the deerskin pants, helping push them down with his bare feet. Then he woke up from his thoughts.

"Oh, De-si-re-e! I've pro-mised-her," Fredrik chanted. Without looking at Tristan, he made a tight bundle from both soiled pieces and tucked it deep inside his dressing trunk standing by the outer wall.

"I must wash and change now. Then I'll send for flowers. She loves my bouquets, Tristan. You should see her smile. Mine—only my bouquets. She truly loves only mine!" Yawned Frederik and dropped on his clean bed.

After that Tristan left the room and returned to his bed.

No, Fred knows nothing at all. Tristan thought. Today, everything felt out of tune. Tristan would have loved to find the long lost note. To be able to go back in time and change the false tune he agreed to orchestrate!

Fred. His young, naive friend. They shouldn't have played with him. He saw it now. They were punished.

Desiree was dead—his beloved girl. He'd give anything to have her letter, to read her words of love she borrowed from Juliet's lines. They recited from Shakespeare together. He knew that scene by heart as well as she did. She was proud of him. She praised him equally for his knowledge, his looks, his tenderness. Tristan had never known such sweet warm love existed. He closed his eyes and tried to picture their last moments together. They flickered in his mind, mixed with all other times, until he fell asleep.

Frederik woke up the next morning a new man. A small song on his lips, a bright spark in his eyes. For the first time Tristan observed they were set far apart like a wild bird of prey.

The Secret Maneuver

Their horses were packed by morning, and off they went towards Burgenland, the southern estates of the Counts of Schönbruck. Frederik never mentioned Desiree again. *True aristocrat.* Tristan admired his young friend's self control.

By midafternoon, they rode in the hills. Forests all around them made the clicking of horseshoes almost inaudible. Tristan was tired.

"How far?"

"Well, not close," Fred replied, an idea forming in his mind. "Let's take a shortcut!"

Tristan yawned. "Thank God."

Frederik turned his horse to a less visible path. It ran under the pine trees and meandered towards a lake visible not far in front. Tristan's horse started following Frederik's. The young Count knew the terrain well. Tristan was too tired and followed his lead. In a few moments the lake was no longer in front of them. Tristan didn't notice.

Leopold opened the heavy tin box sent to him all the way from Innsbruck. His friend Quido von Gloubitz was sending his newspapers by postillion. *Crazy!*

Leopold mentioned casually in his letter that his people here in Brgenland mentioned the murder trial. They are curious. He himself was curious where the thing stood.

The box was full of issues of Quido's newspaper_Der Blatt.

His letter was a several pages long mix of humble observations and boastful hilarity. Leopold had to smile.

He didn't feel like reading the whole story. The top issue caught his eye.

"Desiree Murdered!" Screamed the headline. It was issued only a few days ago.

It turned out that Quido followed the famous actress ever since she first appeared in Innsbruck.

Desiree. One name. A star. It was a pity. She was still young. Leopold didn't know much about Desiree. Frederik mentioned her, and so did his daughter-in-law. Leopold loved books. He preferred to read Shakespeare, Molière, Goethe, and others. Theatre houses didn't hold any appeal for him.

He glanced one more time through Quido's letter. It was the Post Scriptum that stirred things.

In a few sentences von Gloubitz summarized the full case:

"The chief inspector of police was sent back to the theatre. The drunken janitor with a stardom-filled past was his only witness. It's Marius, of great fame, measurable only to Vigano. He was also the only possible suspect! Imagine. In the end they let him go free. The case was put aside for lack of evidence. Pity. That could have sold some issues.

You see, my friend, there was no real document about Desiree. All her papers turned out to be false!

Imagine, Poldi. Not a single line of truth! Nobody could explain anything. It was only when names of her lovers were known that it was clearly understood—it was not in anyone's power to investigate in their direction. The case was closed. If it was not so tragic, I would call it all amusing.

You must know this, Poldi, or have I never mentioned this_ She was the young actress from the postillion.

Remember? I told you about her some years ago. The one with the spinning golden ring with swallows. She was a Bernini. Did I ever tell you? Giovanna Bernini."

Leopold reread the Post Scriptum with mixed feelings. It was clear that he would have to take quick action.

He went to his study and lit his meerschaum. He took a small piece of paper with an address from a secret drawer. From a tin plated box he took a new sheet of writing paper. He placed it carefully on the yellow leather pad.

His quil sharpened he opened the crystal inkwell set in a gilded frame of a simple hunting scene.

Antonin came with Wiener Blatt in the afternoon. The same headlines. Just issued. He left the newspaper in the library. Later in the day Count heard Louisa and her mother's lively talk.

Now he had an important letter to dispatch.

When the messenger arrived at the back door Antonin handed him Count's correspondence with two words_ "Vienna, Urgent!"

They would have been surprised to know that it contained just one word_ Cancel!

Just like Desiree's origin was unknown, there was nothing known about her family. When news about her death appeared in newspapers, there came a letter from Innsbruck to the Viennese police. A local publisher of *The Blatt* newspaper, one Quido von Glaubitz, had claimed that he had it on the highest authority that she was a Bernini—Giovanna Bernini—from the famous family of Italian traveling actors. But it was long after the case was already in the archives. Nobody had ever disputed that.

Her father Marco was found dead in the lower Alps. His horse must have shied from a wild animal and the man fell from the saddle down the slope. A tree-root might have trapped his ankle. They said. He must have hung down over the rocky cliff for weeks. The same newspaper claimed that it was on the Italian border with France; close to the spot called the Hunter's Swig. Nobody seemed to have missed him.

Only the imperial judge, Herr Gottschalk, felt satisfied by the divine justice when he closed the murder case against Marco Bernini.

ACT VI

Napoleon was pushing through all of Europe again. Fredrik was in the academy but already an officer and ready to lead his men, should the necessity arise.

Pristine eiderdown of snow was still thin enough to contour vineyards and the landscape beyond them; more and more snow was coming down in feathery large clusters. Soon the whole garden, the park, and the forests on the horizon would become one vast, white backdrop without an end. Louisa shivered. Book in hand, she kept looking down the tall, narrow window. All of the windows were hung with woven woolen blankets across their bottom half to protect the rooms from cold.

Her mother's voice entered the absolute silence of the slow quiet winter afternoon,

"Come here, Louisa, please."

"Yes, Mama?"

"What is it that you are wearing? I just noticed it."

"Oh, a pin . . . a pretty face pin!"

"Take it off, Louisa. Please. It doesn't belong to you."

"I found it in Fred's room, Mama, but he always—"

"What were you doing in Frederik's room?"

"Reading."

"You go there to read?"

"I miss him."

"How did you find it?"

"I sat down on the carpet to read, but then when I turned on my stomach, I saw—"

"You read on your stomach?"

"Yes, and I saw this . . ."

"Have you thought about your dress?"

The Secret Maneuver

". . .on the floor under his bed. She looks like me, Mama, doesn't she?"

"You will ruin your best clothes if you are not careful." She caught a glimpse of it, "Cheap painting."

"I like it! She looks like—"

"No, she doesn't. You should have more care about your dresses."

"I was reading."

The Countess stretched her arm, and her slim palm turned up. "I will return it to Frederik when he comes home."

"Yes, Mama. I know it's Frederik's. But since he is in the army now, I thought . . . that I could wear it . . . a little."

Her voice trickled like the water from melting icicles on the roof on a sunny winter day.

"I'm waiting."

Louisa took off the pin and placed it in the well of her mother's palm. She didn't feel like reading anymore. Her curtsy was more of a suggestion. The smell of rose water slipped around the door frame like her red woolen winter dress.

Marie-Antonia, Countess von Schönbruck knew well what and whom she was looking at: It was a good portrait of a young actress, pictured here as Viola in the *Twelfth Night*. It was well done. The Countess noticed the high quality right away.

You could buy different ones in front of every major theatre—favorite actresses in their many roles and colorful costumes; smiling, pensive, heroic, coquettish; in hats, turbans, or with hair dramatically meandering in the wind. All that likeness and emotion fitted, more or less skillfully, in the small space of the pin. A small circle or an oval which could be pinned to the lapel or hidden in a pocket. You could get a simple, quick hand-painted one on a metal plate for a few copper kreuzers. Then the price went up for those on velum, the thin deerskin, and you would pay up to ten silver pieces for the finely painted pieces on ivory. There were, of course, the golden, bejeweled ones—hard to even imagine their price. Crazy theatre buffs!

That Frederik was one of them surprised the Countess. It didn't shock her. Youth needs idols. If this innocent infatuation is Frederik's_ be it. She placed the pin on the chest of drawers and rang for her maid.

"Hanne, take this miniature to master Frederik's room."

Hanne curtseyed and turned to leave. She made the first step and turned back. The Countess noticed her changed face.

"What is it, girl?"

Hanne spoke fast on one breath, trying not to inhale any of the words in fear they could somehow permeate her body and harm her.

"This is_this is the lady that came to visit master Frederik."

She finished and almost fainted for lack of oxygen. She was taking loud gulps of air, her cheeks started turning red in blotches.

Spilled loganberries, thought Countess. She needed to know more,"How do you mean?"

"I saw her with him in the park."

"Here?'

"Yes, last autumn they were"—Hanne paused before she decided to continue—"talking."

"What else?"

Now that was a command, and the serve girl knew it.

She was standing there, not knowing what to do. Her Mistress just had enough.

"Hannerle! Out with it!"

"They were kissing, and then they . . . they lay down in the grass."

"That's enough! Give me the pin and leave! Now!"

The girl didn't wait for a second longer. She pressed the burning object back in the countess's palm and, forgetting to curtsy, ran out.

The door closed, the room turned quiet. The Countess crossed to the window to have a better look at the miniature.

Yes. It's undoubtedly the young actress we all went to see in Innsbruck—the one Frederik had fallen for. Poor woman. Yes, her likeness did resemble Louisa. Nonsense! Poor woman . . . murdered. Poor Frederik . . . such bad luck.

The Countess felt a cold shiver running up her arms. She pulled her wide cashmere shawl closer to her body. Large, colorful oriental shapes didn't please her that day. She stood there in deep thought for a moment, then with a sudden burst of anger hurried out.

Marie-Antonia shut the door of her son Frederik's bedroom behind her and leaned her back against it. She looked around the small space.

The boy just hasn't been lucky with his choices. Even his tutor left him! The Countess couldn't believe how unfortunate her oldest boy had been.

It's my fault. Darling Frederik's last letter explained everything— Tristan took away with a young woman! I should have known after Frederik came for his last visit without him. Tristan was ill, he said. Now I know. Who would have guessed? My son is left alone in the city! He has been stuck in the academy until spring. I should write to my old friends. He needs to be in good hands again.

She stepped towards her son's bed and sat down. With his eiderdown pillow in her arms, she pressed her face to the heavy wild aroma of goose-feather dust. The soft satin cover caressed her bare skin.

She loves her boy; regardless of his behavior, his fits, his rude manners, his temper. He is so much like his father. She missed him more than she could have ever openly expressed to him—or to anyone, for that matter.

She would have gladly forgiven his irrational accusations, making her the villain who allowed His father to go to the battle, the one who was responsible for his death. She couldn't be even angry nor annoyed by it all. She covered her eyes with both palms. Her whisper came against her will. She had to hear herself say it,

"Because . . . because he's become his father's very image."

She saw the beloved face from the time she met Carl-Maria as a young woman and was madly in love.

That feeling she would always hold dear to her. She would never smudge it—not even when she heard the truth about her husband's death. She loves him through their Frederik forever.

She lifted the pillow and shook it to bring back its fullness, to calm down her nerves.

A letter flew to the ground.

The Countess didn't pounce to get it. She sat there as fear gripped her shoulders and painfully squeezed her breath out. She didn't open the trifold, she lifted it and looked into it from the side. She saw the signature—"Your Loving Des"

She briskly crumpled it and tossed the paper on the floor. The gilded clock on the chest of drawers chimed half an hour. She lost sense of time. With sudden change in her face Marie-Antonia walked forward, bent down and picked up the crumpled letter and unfolded it. She's Frederik's mother. She's here to protect her child. Like before, her maternal instinct overshadowed all others.

"Frederik, my beloved!"

The Countess stopped reading right there. The bedroom lacked oxygen.

She rapidly turned without purpose, shocked, petrified—not by what she was reading but by her reaction to it.

Jealousy. That's what she was feeling. Pure, painful, self-consuming jealousy she forgot she ever possessed. Self-control was her best asset. It left her in the desert of panic. She must read it. She must make herself do it.

She tried to smooth out the folds with the edge of her palm. Once satisfied with it she started reading:

> "When you left, I couldn't close my eyes, thinking about your proposal.
>
> Fred darling, you are so right. Frederik, dearest, we must go away. No one should stand between us. No one. Tristan is just a silly little boy. You are the man I want. You surely know that.
>
> If your purpose in wooing me is proper and made by a man of honor, then you truly want to marry me. Send me a message tomorrow by a messenger that I will obtain and tell me when and where the marriage ceremony will take place. Then I will meet you there, place my future in your hands, and follow you as my husband through the world. Send me details of when, how . . .

The Countess suddenly realized what it was she was reading—the famous actress Desiree playing a game with a naive young man. She played with her Frederik! Now she is dead... "Suits her well!"

Marie-Antonia's voice was full of accusations and judgement. There was no pity. No compassion.

These sentences were Shakespeare. Word for word. The Countess knew her Shakespeare. This is what Juliet says to Romeo from her balcony. This is what all Juliets say to their Romeos on all stages of the civilized World.

The Countess stopped reading, overwhelmed. She knew her son. Frederik couldn't stand anything that was not only for him. Anything given to him secondhand—he hated. More than hated. He abhorred everything that was not exclusively for him.

Her hand squeezed the paper slowly, carefully to a tight ball this time. She didn't toss it on the floor.

The Countess quickly walked to the white tile stove in the corner. The lighting stone was in its place; she pulled it out the side niche. It took several attempts before she managed to light the incriminating piece of paper; it swirled up angrily toward the chimney, then ascended back to the stove. She stood there and watched it burn to ashes.

Only then she closed the heavy little iron door and turned. She needed to lean her forehead on the pale yellow wall for support. Both hands pressed over her mouth she stood there in silence.

Her movements became suddenly hectic. She was progressing from one side of the room to the other. She opened the few drawers. Then all was out, turned up like autumn fields. She didn't find anything else unusual, nothing at all.

Exhausted, she sat down on the carpet. She had commanded herself not to sob. Tears didn't ask her—they were coming down her face silently. She had no strength to deal with them.

The day outside was as jolly as they can be in the hills where the air was so clear above vineyards that distances seem to vanish, everything sitting at your hand's reach. The fresh snow glittered against deep blue skies. Only a hawk was gliding in the translucent air scanning the pristine ground for one unlucky being.

ACT VII

Spring had dried out all roads, yet the Schönbrucks decided to stay in their Burgenland estate till summer.

Louisa left for Vienna with her mother; an invitation was issued from the young man's family to come and enjoy the colorful new premier at the opera house. Frederik joined them in town. Louisa couldn't believe how courteous he'd become, how manly. He was now a real hussar. His braids were meticulously, tightly braided. The blue sashes on their ends were spotless. His thin mustaches glossed with pomade.

He kissed his mother's cheeks and her hand. He bowed to honor her; she blushed against her will. He kissed both of Louisa's hands and both cheeks. *A true nobleman*, she thought for a moment. He was respectful of the other ladies and the dragoon—an ancient Viennese family, high standing in society, tied to the court of Emperor Leopold II. Louisa's future was in making.

When lights went down in the house, Frederik bent and kissed Louisa's bare nape above her golden necklace. She didn't dare to move. Only after the curtain opened and the sudden stream of light from the stage lit faces of the audience did she look at him.

Frederik was watching—no ripple of thought or emotion in his face, no hint of what happened.

After the performance, he accompanied them to their coach.

Once their new acquaintances left, Louisa turned towards him and whispered, "Why?"

But their alert, inquisitive mother asked, "Why? Why what?"

_and made them both invent a lie as if they were ten years old again, both in wide pantaloons playing in the meadow.

On the evening after they came back, Louisa found Leopold alone in the library.

"May I come in?"

"Louisa my dear, you're back! Do come in, please! How was the opera?" He closed his book.

"Opa, I have a dilemma."

"I cannot help you if you don't like opera anymore," His light joke fell flat.

Then he recognized his mistake and without any apology continued down the most logical path.

"If that's about the young man asking your hand in marriage . . ."

"Oh, him. No. Yes, of course. I . . . I truly like him."

"But?"

"But there's something else."

Leopold's mind was startled. *Something else? She's not sure now?* He opened his book again and started playing with the red leather bookmark. He was too unprepared to be an adviser in Louisa's matters of the heart. *No, I can't do this.*

"I can't do this," Leopold said quickly, "Tell your mother"

"I cannot . . . it's just my . . ." Louisa was at the end of inventing a story. *He doesn't deserve this.*

"What? Are you talking about your daydreams?"

He would have sworn that she was lying.

"It's too complicated. I see it now, I'm sorry."

"Can you talk to him?"

"I've tried, I have, I mean . . . I really . . ."

"Well, then perhaps, as I said, your mother could help you better than I can, my dear."

Louisa heard the uncharacteristic impatient undertone. She didn't want to hurt him, but she couldn't tell him the truth either—not that day anyways.

"That's all right. I . . . I will think of something."

Leopold registered her hesitation, "Is there anything else?"

He watched her closely as she looked at him. Her eyes seemed to hold to his for an extra second. Her smile couldn't override sadness, which colored her irises. They turned a shade darker before she curtseyed and left.

Her silk, satin dress made the sound around the doorframe, which to his ears sounded suddenly like silk sheets early in the morning before the first birds brighten up the fresh morning air, when bodies find each other, when senses wake up in the midst of perpetual choreography which inspires new movements, fresh emotions, surprising truth reborn every time lovers wake up in each other's arms.

This was madness. Leopold reached for the small bell and rang it with unexpected frustration.

Skies were unwillingly changing the dark to lighter tones of blue. Early-morning fresh air surprised Leopold's face as he opened the window. He could hear dogs being taken from the zwinger and all was packed for the hunting trip.

His command came late at night, but everything was prepared as usual. His setters rushed in and were dancing around their master.

They always know first, don't they? the Count marveled.

Once he gave command "go!" his dogs squeezed around him. Their slender but heavily built bodies pushed him to the side towards the doorframe; they rushed down the corridor joyfully. He gave a muted whistle only he could do. Dogs were back in a flesh meandering their bodies around their beloved Master.

Antonin appeared on top of the stairs.

"We are ready, my lord."

He handed Leopold a tall walking stick. Deep notches in the stem reported times Leopold shot an elk. The three carved rings on its top were for bears.

Antonin's chest was crisscrossed with ammunition and two short horns with brass mouthpiece. He handed one to Leopold who barely resisted blowing it at this hour.

"Off to the hills!" he declared.

"How is my Louisa today?!" called Count von Schönbruck jovially from the hallway before he stepped into Louisa's bedroom.

He cleared his mind in the crisp, fragrant air in the forests of Burgenland. He had several days to organize his mind, to reposition his emotions, to be back as the grandfather, Opapa, Opa, as he always aspired to be.

He hoped to see Louisa that day; the deep pockets of his hunting jacket carried some lovely things, many of them he picked expressly for his favorite granddaughter.

He stopped to give gifts to all his younger grandchildren already. The hunting expedition was a great success. The large chip of a pale agate he picked up when crossing the shallow stream was truly exquisite. He thought he would present that one to Louisa after dinner when the whole family would be around.

Only a few minutes ago, he was disturbed by his valet in the library. The Countess wanted to talk to him. She was in her daughter's room.

Would the Count come at once? Now he feared that Louisa fell ill. That explained why he hadn't seen her yet that day. He took the last several steps two at a time.

Marie-Antonia, Countess von Schönbruck, his daughter-in-law, closed the door behind him the second he walked in.

"Louisa is not here..."

He saw her face, the look in her violet eyes.

She stretched her slender arm with a piece of paper. It trembled as she handed it to him.

"Read . . . please."

She covered her face with the overlay of her white dress. She didn't cry. She stood there like a Greek statue, like one of those he and Louisa used to admire in the large book.

"What?"

Count's mind was slowly coming into realization that *that* was kind of an emergency.

"Louisa . . . she . . . I think that she . . ." Countess von Schönbruck hesitated.

"Eloped!" Leopold was quick to guess.

Count's face had changed in front of his shocked daughter-in-law. His voice erupted in the speed which she found impossible to interrupt, "How infantile! To run away! To . . ."

"No! Please, calm down, Father. No, no! It's worse . . . much worse."

Leopold looked at her puzzled. "What could be worse?" He tried to speak patiently.

The suspense didn't sit well with him" What?"

"It looks like she . . . drowned herself."

Count's mind went mute. He felt nothing. The room changed its shape, its length, its height; and then came back at him like a wild horse injured in the midst of a battlefield.

He was still a strong man and didn't fall. He didn't sit down. He couldn't speak. He listened.

"There was her shawl, the one you gave her, the silk one, by the river_" the young Countess said quickly.

Her voice suspended that sentence in the air between them, not finishing it with a full stop, not lowering it into a closure.

Was there a question mark in her mind? Was there an exclamation point?

He couldn't tell.

She took a sudden, loud deep breath; her voice quivered. She leaned forward and grasped Leopold's arm to keep herself steady.

The Count, himself speechless and forlorn, stood there stricken, in shock. He placed Louisa's scarf over his shoulder and put his hand on his daughter-in-law's forearm. They remained in silence.

The gilded clock on the secretary struck one time to announce a quarter of the upcoming hour. He felt his daughter-in-law's body growing heavy on his arm. Leopold guided her to the chair that looked as fragile as the grieving young woman herself.

She slid on it and clutched the sides of its ebony frame with long thin fingers full of mourning rings. The tender knuckles of her long fingers turned pale.

Leopold knelt down in front of her.

"Did they find her?" he asked this, although he knew that it was impossible. The river here never gave back what she took.

The Countess shook her head no. *Of course not.*

"Who discovered the scarf?"

"Our boys did. They played down there. I had come here to give her the scarf and found the note. Then I sent for you."

"Yes . . . yes. That was good."

He was trying to think, not to panic.

He took Louisa's note from the short cherrywood side table where he absentmindedly placed it. His pince-nez on he started reading out loud: "Goodbye, all I love—now I truly must go!"

He stood up disturbed, walked to the window, and turned towards the room. He stayed there, organizing wild images into a steady stream of reason. Then he crossed back, pulled the second chair towards her, and sat down. When she turned her head to look him in the face, she saw in it a clear plan. He didn't fail her.

"First, no one must know." Leopold folded the note and tucked it inside his vest. "No one."

It had the sound of a military order. He was the highest charge here.

The young Countess understood her father-in-law's intentions—though everything else was beyond reach of her grieving horror-stricken mind.

Tears in her voice, she tried to grasp his plan. "But how? How are we going to survive . . . all . . . all of this?"

"We must. We will say that she came back from her walk unwell."

The Count stood up and started pacing to and fro.

"She's ill! She's in bed. It's infectious! I don't know . . . she contracted . . . yes! Infectious fever—no, she's got German measles! That's it! Everyone must leave. Immediately! Now! Yes, German measles!"

With new energy, he started dictating his plan, which was coming to him clearer as he was presenting it to her.

"Tell everyone, pack the children, all must leave quickly! Go, take them back to Innsbruck!"

He stood up, his muscles already on alert.

"I must send a messenger to the abbey. The bishop was supposed to have dinner with us next Thursday. I will dispatch some letters. I must stay behind. I'll stage her trip to a spa, somewhere at the seaside. I'll take her to the Baltic! We will mourn her after everyone receives our letter of her . . ."

He avoided saying *death*.

"Her . . . of her . . ."

He couldn't choose a word.

He bent towards Marie-Antonia and gently squeezed her shoulder.

"We must start, my dear. Now. Tell the nannies. Send notes to Frau Ebner, to Thomas—to everyone."

The Countess's brain was trying hard to follow and to be present.

"No one must come here into the house! I'll take care of my valets. They'll travel with you."

His mind was running like his horse used to—in full gallop.

"We must do this!"

As if his proposition needed more weight, he slowed down his speech.

"For our family's sake, we have to do it! You understand? All your children's prospects will be ruined if we don't."

That suddenly woke her up.

"My children! Yes! My darling poor children!"

As she turned to him, her face changed. Now both hands clasped the shawl she wore around her shoulders.

She was pulling it down as she started shouting in a muffled voice, "How could she be so cruel! Not thinking about the children!"

Her anger shocked him. From a mourning mother, she turned into a vicious wild animal guarding her cubs.

"What selfish . . ." tears in her voice smudged the next word.

A few moments later, she rushed out the door. To his relief, Leopold heard her calling out loud to all maids, nannies, and children in quick succession. Her voice became steady, decisive. She was the firm mistress of her household as ever.

There was war again. Napoleon invaded Vienna after the Austrians attacked! He made a clear cut behind any peace in

Austerlitz. British attacked French fleets. Napoleon's demands swept the political scene of Europe, turning regular folks' lives upside down. Order was uprooted. Chaos ruled.

His invasion of Tyrol left everyone speechless. He did something unprecedented. He gave orders to protect the enormous, important collections gathered for centuries in the Ambras Castle. That was the fine education he received in France, which his noble parents lavished on him. His father's years at the French court as the Ambassador of Corsica at Versailles surely brushed on his cultured manners that made him see with clarity what loss for humanity would have happened. Tyrolean nobility exhaled. Leopold was one of them.

The army was everywhere. Passports and paperwork all were examined too often, making travels almost impossible. But Count von Schönbruck was in no hurry back home. He progressed slowly down from the Baltic until he finally arrived at Burgenland. He smelled the air. No salt in it like up north. Fresh, sweet, round.

Down along the river, through his rolling hills, up among the vineyards—he was home.

It was understood by all that Louisa didn't survive her illness, that she was buried up in Prussia by the sea. She was mourned. Cried after. Magdalena Ebner was inconsolable.

The Countess changed back to colors of mourning. Her children observed with sadness how she withdrew from life again.

Louisa's brother Frederik sent his messenger with the largest bouquet of flowers anybody had ever seen in Burgenland. It was almost vulgar. They discarded it before Leopold returned. Requiem Mass was held only in Innsbruck due to the war. Marie-Antonia's confessor turned more introverted than ever before.

Autumn was approaching. Vineyards were turning vine leaves red and purple. The first frost will curl them in, shrivel the grapes left behind to make ice wine and raisins. The mist spread low among the strict lines of vineyards. Rose shrubs had lost leaves but had an abundance of hops to make birds happy all winter.

Count von Schönbruck waited until the corridor was left clear of his valet's steps. Only then he walked carefully to the other side of his library, filled up a brilliantly cut crystal glass to its rim, and took a careful sip.

Recently he got into the habit of refilling it way too often. He could tell from Antonin's look.

Leopold opened his palm. A small, short pencil was warm from his grip.

It was the one he found in Louisa's room the day she disappeared. It was a good fit with the pencil holder on Louisa's silver chatelaine. He hung it around his neck. As if it could reveal its secret to him, as if he could speak to Louisa through it, he held the little stump close to his lips.

"Why? Why were you hiding it under your pillow? It doesn't make any sense. Where is all that which you were writing with it?"

He had been going mad over this detail for almost a year! And then there was the other mystery—Louisa's goodbye note! The note she'd left written in ink was so meticulous, not a shaky hand of someone who decides to do such a desperate, mad act.

It all began making less and less sense to him. Pictures in front of his inner eye started moving like clouds chased by high winds. Seasons had changed. He was looking over his desk out the window. The wind was blowing down colored leaves from tree crowns. Drops of early autumn rain hit the window panes. He noticed a split tree branch twisted by a strong gust. The exposed wood was light with long, dark marks.

Count pushed himself back from his desk. He swiveled to the left and reached in front of him. One of the slim, vertical secret drawers was built inconspicuously into colorful inlays of exotic, rare bright-colored wood of his secretary. The inner spring mechanism tossed out a thin cassette. Count helped it out and turned it upside down. He shook it, hit it several times against his dry palm until the edge of Louisa's note appeared.

His mind was calm. His eyes focused without veils of tears.

Only today he was able to truly look at it. Louisa's final goodbye—not for him, not for anyone. It was written in sepia. He took out his magnifying glass with a malachite handle. The one she would always admire.

Louisa's handwriting was undisturbed. She modeled each letter with care and precision. Each line ended in swirling arabesques done with finesse beyond her sixteen years. All were even, precisely executed strokes. This could not be a goodbye of someone going to her own death.

He stood up with complete conviction. He turned to his image in the looking glass.

"No, she did not!"

Feeling empowered by his double presence, he said hesitantly, "Louisa was . . .!" But he couldn't make himself finish the horrid sentence. There was still the "What if." He decided to hold tight to it.

Leopold was out with a few large steps. He almost collided with his valet.

Antonin, his arm stretched, was handing him _was it a note?

"Not now."

"But my wife thinks it's important, my lord."

Leopold pulled it from his man's fingers and glanced at it.

"She found it as she was cleaning. . ."

Leopold's world shook. He heard blood pounding in his ears. He turned and walked to his desk.

His fingers stretched the paper most tenderly.

It was a poem. Louisa's brilliant wrist, as she had learned calligraphy from her governess, twisted and meandered words of love and hope. Seemingly free but tightly disciplined strokes of her pen gifted the sheet of paper with emotional wealth of her mind. It was all positive and hopeful—a goodbye to her childhood, her joyful greetings of her youth. It had everything he cherished in her. Here was her childish naivete, sense of humor, intelligence:

> Goodbye, Robinson, Goodbye, Friday,
> I must be off, won't see you on Monday,
> Without you, my beloved games, my nursery play.
> Don't try to stop me, I bid you farewell.
> Hear sounds of the bells of my happiness and pray
> My impatient heart is brimming with joy.

The paper was folded and torn there. He put the note that was left—her presumed suicide letter—next to the paper. It fit perfectly :

Goodbye, all I love! Now I truly must go.

The light changed behind the window. It was overcast. Leopold watched a flock of birds absorbing another. His blood stopped rushing. The flock must have multiplied to thousands.

There was no sorrow like this one. He lost his love twice. His life was done.

There was no way to find a murderer. Not even think that someone would be interested at the time of looming war to do so.

His scheme to cover up Louisa's disappearance seemed like an extremely bad joke. All the trouble, all the expense. Just because the world is intolerant. Cruel.

Under his madness there was a thin streak of hope.

Now he knew that his beloved Louisa didn't take her own life. He was convinced that she wouldn't have eloped. Although the third possibility was so grim, deep in his soul he'd preferred that to Louisa being with another man.

What had Louisa written with her pencil secretly placed under her pillow? Where is that writing? Why? Is it a diary?

Probably. If she went away she took it, no doubt. But if he finds it...

His body was shivering. Count returned to his bed, called Antonin, and asked for a strong broth with just a small glass of Tokaji in it.

Count hated dreams. The one he woke up from was different. In it he found Louisa. She didn't speak to him but seemed happy and tempted him to follow her down to the river. There her image evaporated.

The next morning, Leopold walked down through the vineyards all the way to the vast river. He could relax and breathe there again. Such a monumental flow—majestic, quick, strong in the most inconspicuous way. The surface almost always looks like a mirror. He watched the flow. How different it was from his brisk river up in the Alps! He decided to stay in Burgenland until he knew the whole truth. Then he'll bring her home. Or her murderer to justice.

He swore it to the river; he was certain that she listened. He was watching colorful ducks, a small group of young storks, and a blue heron fishing. Louisa always loved this view. He turned and started walking along the river; the path under the old, tall willow trees was overgrown with grasses. Something glistened on the ground. He bent down.

Neh, just a small button from a military uniform.

He picked it up, nevertheless. Habitually, more than out of interest, he put it in one of his many pockets.

For the first time in months, he thought about his grandchildren. He missed them. His steps moved into a jog up the hill. There were letters to write.

Count von Schönbruck was sitting at his desk. He couldn't decide whether to write his daughter-in-law the truth. He decided not to. Although these were modern times, the difference between suicide and elopement was nil, as far as the family ruin was concerned. He wouldn't dare to mention the last alternative to her. She found her peace by now, although she returned to mourning colors of her wardrobe.

He wrote, however, to both his solicitors. He then sealed the two envelopes.

On their front, he wrote: "To Be Opened Only in Case of My Death." Each was then inserted into a larger envelope and sealed again.

With the big burden off his shoulders, he sat there without a thought. Then it was all rudimental. He rang the brass bell, and his Antonin came in.

"I am hungry, my dear man."

Antonin smiled. *Perhaps times are going to change for the better.*

"Bring me speck and bread, some cheese, and a bottle of Veltlin."

"Anything else?"

"Send a message to the cook—duck for tomorrow, red cabbage, and dumplings."

Antonin bowed, and his step got a different spring to it. For the first time in months, Leopold regretted that Magdalena Ebner was sent to Innsbruck. *Poor Lena!* Thomas married the head-forester's daughter. At least that went smoothly; no need for any replacements. Leopold lit his meerschaum. His estate, his people. All was ticking as always, the way he liked it.

Leopold slapped his desk with the latest letter from Quido. No results. No sign of Louisa. It all looked so hopeful, then went awry again. Winter was cold. Vineyards rested happily under muffs of snow. There was scarce news from the army. Frederik was somewhere in Europe, preparing to fight.

Spring found Leopold's questions still unanswered. He kept looking, without losing his mind.

He had tried to enjoy the weather as much as he could but the hollow feeling of void was too painful. His guilt and his desperation had reigned over his days and nights. He scavenged through the whole house.

Nothing.

He hung the small pencil around his neck.

Hot summer arrived with storms; and days turned to sultry, oppressive boxes of nothingness. The wine cellar was the place to be.

Napoleon crowned himself the emperor last winter. He hoped for the ancient title of the Holy Roman Emperor, but in a brilliant move, that title was dissolved! That made everybody in the Austrian Empire laugh! Napoleon must have been furious. He was crowned King of Italy next as a consolation prize. It was all madness.

Leopold had nothing else on his mind but how to find Luisa's whereabouts. He sent more letters than ever. None held any new information.

He ignored letters from his daughter-in-law about Frederik's success in battles, her hints on the secret maneuver he never taught him. It annoyed him all over again. After that, he would archive every letter from Marie-Antonia without ever opening it.

He had pushed everything and everyone in the periphery of his hazy, monochromatic existence of late.

By the end of summer, Austria joined the latest coalition. Leopold Count von Schönbruck had heard that plans for an October battle were in the making. Another autumn without enough men for the harvest.

Leopold poured himself the large, heavy gilded glass full of red. He lifted the delicious liquid against the window. The day out there turned bloody red.

The library—he hasn't been there for some time now. It had always been the best place to recuperate from all sorts of ailments. The library was where Leopold had lived most of the time, all his adult life. He couldn't reconcile with the fact that he had forgotten! He would spend hours browsing. Hours reading with Louisa.

When he walked in, he looked at the books sitting around the room. He took them out the last time. Now he remembered, nothing was able to truly amuse him.

He returned to Rousseau, reread Voltaire, and not even his friend Goethe was able to bring him solace.

How about today?

He was standing there, glass half full in his hand, his head turned sideways.

His eyes were probing volume after volume, his memory recalling sentences, and then there was the *Robinson Crusoe* he gifted Louisa.

She loved it right away. She embraced the story despite the raised eyebrows around her. Books for boys, books for girls—he never could understand. His only division was good books and bad books.

He knew the story almost by heart. It made him smile.

"Daniel Defoe, Robinson Crusoe," he said out loud as if he was a young boy again.

It had brought him pleasure always, and he was certain it wouldn't fail him today.

Anytime he opened it, as if an old friend came calling.

Sunshine suddenly brightened up the terrace; he could go and read out there. Count von Schönbruck walked out. The terrace was cleanly swept. A group of wicker chairs waited for guests, all in bright sunshine, unaware of the state of the world beyond the balustrade.

Leopold pulled the wicker armchair and sat down on cushions of colorful chintz stuffed with dry forest grass. He held the book in his arms; his palms enjoying the volume and its soft cover. He bent his head, and the familiar scent seduced his senses.

When he opened his eyes, sometime later, his face was splashed with water. His first thoughts were his grandchildren. That was something they would tease him with when he dozed off like that in the midafternoon. He forgot—they were all with their mother in Innsbruck!

He glanced around. The sun was shining, but tiles and the ground around the terrace were steaming, permeating a fresh, peppery scent after a brief shower.

Count shook his wet mane with streaks of gray. *Old dog!* He heard von Gloubitz's voice in his head. It couldn't reach his funny bone today. Leopold outstretched his arm. He lifted the book which slid down from his legs. He held it away from his body and saw how wet it was.

How stupid of me!

He heard his father's voice calling impatiently: "No books out of the library! Can you hear me!"

He stood up, and__Louisa's volume fell on the ground. It too was soaked.

"Oh, great."

Leopold bent to pick it up and stopped, confused.

The book looked like a cacti, a unique species of desert. Pages were multiplied and held stiff to all directions.

Count couldn't comprehend what he was looking at—then it became suddenly clear. The rain washed away some kind of glue which held the pages stuck together close to the binding.

He put the book back on his lap, his pince-nez securely on top of his nose. His impatience guided his hands. He very carefully inserted his fingers in between pages and pulled.

In front of Leopold's eyes, a new world opened up to him like sets of secret rooms.

Alongside the binding, drawn up and down, were some sort of ornaments. He lifted the book closer to his eyes and immediately recognized his mistake.

Those were not arabesques imitating old manuscripts as he'd erroneously estimated.

He turned the book to its side—he was looking at the pencil-written text in Louisa's handwriting.

Leopold moved inside the library as quickly as he was able to. Then he locked the door and sank down in his low armchair.

Some of the pages were still stuck together; but some, closer to the covers, were already giving up their contents. Leopold's fingers held down a random page.

"I love him!" he read aloud.

Shocked by a sudden new wave of his own jealousy, he closed the book.

He was holding the truth, but he wasn't ready for it. Never before did he experience layers of anger like now; they threatened to make him break something tangible, to hit the blue wall with that white vase Louisa used to bring him wildflowers for.

I must calm down. I'm too old for letting my emotions get the best of me.

He reopened the book.

> I do love him! I didn't know it until recently . . . no, not true. I've known it all my life, for he's part of me. He's my blood, my soul, my thoughts, my heart. He is the man I want, one whom I admire the most, the man I want to be with my whole life.

A knock on the door interrupted his thoughts. It was concerned Franz.

"Go away! I don't wish to be disturbed! Tell everyone!"

Count poured some slivovitz into a small green glass. He returned to his armchair and took a swig.

With a slight buzz in his head, he leafed through the book randomly, where more pages had already opened up and allowed him to read.

He'd cry so much, and it was heartbreaking, just like when his Duchess was killed . . . just like when I found my little doll Miechen. Such a softhearted boy, he is. Why does he have to go to the army?

"Because he wanted to!" Shouted Leopold.

Yes, he always wanted to. Ever since he was a little boy, in the saddle in front of his father. He was ready for combat.

My heart hurts for him . . .

Leopold read aloud, his eyes widened. "This can't be! She's in love with . . . Frederik?"

He reopened the book at his first point of reading;

> I cannot imagine my life without him . . . ever. He's taught me everything I know. Since I can remember, probably since I was born. . .

She's in love with him deeply, dangerously. She idolizes him! Leopold began recalling their childhood. Fred and Louisa.

Their youth, growing up together, their holding hands, running to the forest—it was making more and more sense. In front of his eyes, a god-forbidden, tragic new existence started to take shape. This can't be.

She's been living tucked away in army barracks with Fred! Count stood up and walked across the room, the book in his hands. He was shocked, grief-stricken, appalled, jealous. Empathetic. He must bring them back. He must let them know that he forgave them. That they can . . .

He is their grandfather. He will help them. He stopped and leaned his back against the window frame. He made himself go and read the whole truth.

Several more pages popped open, he jumped readily in to learn more.

But he wasn't prepared for anything like what came next:

> . . . I know Frederik is going to kill me, he said so.

Leopold had to sit down. He drank water straight from the jug. It was as cold as a blade.

> He said first how much we've always loved each other, that I always belonged to him, that it's the only way. But I can't love him the way he wants me to . . . he said he would kill me, just like he killed my Mieschen and his Duchess. He thought I would be frightened and let him come to my bed at night.

Leopold's hands started trembling as he clutched the book, his eyes were rushing forward like his blood.

He read Louisa's worries written in her earlier handwriting.

> I cannot tell anyone. He's my brother, my own blood. I still love him, but I fear! I tried to reason with him earlier, he went mad! I'm scared. So scared. I don't know what to do. I don't want to tell on him.

Leopold's thumbs ripped open another page still glued together:

> I didn't tell him anything more about my true love, but it's enough what he knows already to kill me. He told me how he stabbed Tristan in the forest, that he betrayed him with Desiree. He killed her first and he stole a ring from her, a ring with swallows.

Count's eyes stayed over the last sentence. He stood up in sudden urge to run. The overwhelming wave of angry sorrow almost paralyzed him. His fingers tried to tear open the remaining pages. It was not as easy. The glue was strong and old. Narrow, lozenge-shaped views to Louisa's secrets opened. Fragments couldn't satisfy his rush, his need for truth:

> *But my true deep love belongs to__*

"To whom?" screamed Leopold.

He cut his fingers as he hectically ripped the pages, his blood started smudging over the paper.

More struggle _ and there was his answer:

> ...*Fred says he'll give me one last chance. Maybe this is all I can ever say, Opa!*
> *I am frightened! I will tell Fred if it's the last thing I'll say in this strange, complicated world. Leopold! Love! My Love. My only, My greatest LOVE! I love you with all my body and soul my dearest, my beloved. You taught me to give my heart only to the one who's worthy. My heart is yours, Leopold! Forever! I hear steps Adieu Love! I___*

Leopold's eyes froze on the last sentence. He sat there, holding his breath as if he could accidentally blow away those perplexing, utterly unbelievable words—his greatest secret dream-come-true. His unspeakable sorrow, happiness that had reversed itself into a vanishing point.

When Leopold reached for his sword, he didn't know how much time had passed. He didn't remember how he got outside. His head was spinning; but he started running, looking for Frederik, to find him, to punish him, to kill him.

His vengeance combusted to flame; his jealousy had mixed with pain into hellish, sickening mud, filling his veins, his eyes, his brain.

Frederik! You are dead!

He felt as if his roar shook the whole estate. Only that his voice never slipped over the threshold of his lips, bitten to shreds by now; all that time he remained silent, his throat turned raw and hoarse with sorrow. His heart burned to cinders—he stopped, exhausted, as nausea tried to overpower him.

He knelt down among tufts of tall grass and bent to the ground; his head rested on the cool soil. The strong smell like steel of blade filled up his senses. He waited, hidden in the meadow, until his world stopped spinning backwards. Only then he remembered that Frederik was not coming home till tomorrow, straight from the battlefield.

The Secret Maneuver

Leopold, Count von Schönbruck sat by the fire all night. He allowed Franz to bring him more wine and a few bites of bread. He slept in the armchair wrapped in Louisa's silk shawl, clutching her book.

Before morning, he got chills and had to call in servants to make fire in the tall green stove. He pressed his back on the tiles. The glossy squares started warming up. His shivers eventually ceased, and he closed eyes but couldn't stop his thoughts.

The army town from where the note from Fred was dispatched was roughly two days in the saddle. He might be quicker, though, and get there by noon that day. God only knows if he still had his own horse or some battlefield trade-off.

The strong red from his vineyards started having the effect he hoped for. Count walked back to his armchair and, holding Louisa's book against his chest, fell asleep almost the moment he merged into the green velvet upholstery.

The next day, he woke up in panic that he overslept. He rushed to the small window. Men in the park were progressing with their scythes in the field of blooming grasses. By the decapitated stalks, he could guess that it was not yet midmorning.

A small figure of a horse galloping towards the chateau appeared at the end of the oak alley.

Clouds of dust rolling on both sides of the strong, gracious black animal were getting closer. In the saddle—a hussar in full garb!

It took the Count a few more moments to be sure; then he recognized colors of the regiment. Frederik was home.

Count took just one more glance at Louisa's writing. He needed to see the words, her handwriting, to be with her, hear her voice—to brand her perplexing, sweet confessions freshly into mind, to have her love for him within his love for her, to carry her with him through his most difficult task.

He tucked the book inside his jacket's breast plate. He reached for her shawl, and picked up his sword as he rushed out the door.

Now was a new day. Count von Schönbruck yelled down the corridor. His voice was shattering window panes, sending wood chips flying from balustrades and gables. He wasn't thinking about anything but one.

"Frederik! Come here! At once!"

Franz, barely catching up with his master's speed, hurried to tell him that the young Count went immediately towards the river.

"I'll kill him!"

But he knew it was not as straightforward as he made it sound.

Morning was quickly getting old. The sun was mixing with clouds. The warmth was already laced with sharp cold streaks heralding autumn.

Count was pacing with large strokes, ignoring meandering river-rock paved pathways. He was strutting straight through the garden, through the small vineyard, in the direction of the river. His mind was rushing with him.

Fred must do what this ancient family's honor requires of him, of his name, of his father's memory. He has to go and confess!

Leopold's eyes were foggy from lack of sleep, his face unshaven. Blotches of gray and black dotted his chin. His face was washed white; his throat choked on the word *murderer*; yet it was this word that pushed him into an unevenly paced jog.

Frederik must be called to justice! He must be punished…he… must…

Count's thoughts cleared up; he stopped. While catching his breath, he knew this was a stalemate. None of the above was possible, precisely for that very same reason—such a scandal would have destroyed this family, all of its members, now and in the future. Forever.

Leopold turned. Franz must have talked. They all walked behind him—Antonin, his wife, their little boy, the cook and her help, and several men from vineyards—like a crowd of somnambulists following blindly the full moon, like mice following Pieter Piper.

No! I can't have them here!

His left arm shot out, and remnants of his index finger pointed at the house. Without trying to connect with them any further, Count hurried forward. He didn't see them as they stayed at that very spot like a voiceless Greek chorus.

One more alley of oaks, one more curve, and a sudden steady roar of water down below made him glance down.

Frederik was standing under the steep overhang, still in his full hussar's uniform—deep in thoughts, his head bent down.

Count von Schönbruck jumped the rocky slope to get closer. As if carving the horrid sentence in a block of ice up in the mountains, he kept repeating for himself *Guilty! Frederik's guilty! He murdered my Louisa! This is the end.*

He took a deep breath.

"Frederik!"

Frederik didn't move. It was only when his grandfather stood in front of him that he looked up. He saw immediately that the Count was wearing Louisa's shawl across his chest, his sword hanging from it as if it was his baldric.

Frederik's cheeks turned red, but he didn't budge. Instead, he turned his face up to his grandfather.

"What do you want with me, Opa? What are you coming to bug me with here, Old-pa? You son of a bi—"

"Don't talk to me like that, sir."

The Count's index finger shot forward; and were it a blade, it would have slashed Frederik's face. Instead, it stopped an inch from his battlefield-dust-covered skin. The face belonged to a man of indifferent age, as war evens out all men: narrow, bloodshot, pale eyes; one eyebrow burnt half off; his long hair in thin hussar braids, their ends tied with dirty blue sashes, heavy with fat and dust; his dry lips under blade-thin mustache measured the rhythm of victory.

"I'll talk to you as I choose, for you have no power over me anymore!"

Count von Schönbruck was looking at his grandson, his heir. But their little Frederik, a freshly issued war hero, was a different man. His mind left him. His unshaved chin moved forward.

"You had hots for her, Opa, didn't you? You old goat! You disgust me!"

He spat on the ground in front of Leopold.

His head bent to the side, and his thin braids swayed. One got caught across his mouth, he spat it out angrily. His voice shifted into a higher pitch of ridicule.

"You old, shaky Satyre who lost his tail!"

"Frederik, don't."

"She told me everything! She was no good! Just like the others! I loved her, and she always, always loved me! Only me! What did you do to her? What charms did you use, what potions? What gifts did you give her that she turned away from me?"

There was nothing to save this child with, yet Leopold, his grandfather, tried.

"Frederik, listen, come home with me now. I know."

But his grandson was far deeper inside his own misery.

"You never gave me anything that counts . . . none of you! Even my papa! He was all mine, and he too left me, like all the others! Like everybody I'd ever loved!"

His tears were leaving light streaks in the dust as they started flooding his face.

"Even Tristan!" Frederik's eyes looked up to the sky. "They thought I was stupid. He even carried her letter around!"

Shreds of his laughter resembled hiccups.

"My Des! She was only mine! I had to kill him, you see, but first my Desiree—she was mine! She said so . . . only mine!"

Fred hit his chest and rested his left hand on the soiled jacket. There was the ring with swallows on his grandson's dirty finger. Frederik stepped close to his grandfather, almost touching him.

Leopold didn't move. His green eyes didn't miss any of Frederik's gestures.

"Louisa hated you! She told me. Ha! She couldn't stand you!"

He pushed the Count away from him with a strong bump of his chest. He was immediately ready to fight; the naked sword suddenly in hand.

"Did you have fun with her? Did she please your old bones?"

Count's sword flew out to his hand, "Shut up! You need a doctor."

"I need a doctor? That's thick. It's you . . . you'll need a doctor to pronounce you dead once I'm finished with you!"

The Secret Maneuver

Frederik charged forward and missed. His anger turned his dusty face almost purple. Fury inundated his mind.

It was beyond him to detect the change that happened here:

The man in front of him was no longer his grandfather—despite what his eyes were telling Frederik; this man was Leopold, Count von Schönbruck, a young man in love.

"Fight with me! Fight!" Frederik's screams shook his whole body as he shouted on top of his lungs,

"She called your name! To her last breath, she kept calling your name!"

Leopold turned away, for tears engulfed his eyes. His back hunched to conceal his sorrow.

There was not enough time to think, but it was enough for Frederik. He attacked him from behind!

What happened next happened in a fraction of the next second, between two blinks of an eye. There was not a known block for that clever maneuver, but the little boy, hidden in the safety of his mother's skirts, watching, didn't know that.

The secret maneuver was there to have, to save one's life.

It could have saved Leopold's in Adige, at times when he called himself Georg. He didn't wait for that chance to happen. He despised fistfights, especially with someone of lower rank. He killed Giovanna's unarmed cousin Gab before the jealous young actor had time to attack him. The secret maneuver had been a deadly move, without exception. It didn't shun talent. It had little care for age. It was final.

EPILOGUE

Leopold Count von Schönbruck was walking slowly forward, one careful step placed in front of the other. His thighs were pushing through the heavy water, he was making his way deeper into the middle of the river.

He carried his dead grandson close to his chest, just like when Frederik was a little boy and he taught him to swim.

Count knew his river well; he could be sure that she would forgive him. She would welcome the two murderers without questioning.

His walk slowed down as Frederik's soaked uniform was weighing him down. But he didn't stop moving. The emerald-green water started lifting his body. Leopold held Frederik tightly until the undercurrents became too quick.

Attached to him by his belt, he kissed the hereditary Count von Schönbruck and moved further into the deep. . .

Only now he started thinking of Louisa again. His love was with him—her scarf across his chest, her book inside his jacket. He looked up to the skies. Swallows in large flocks were crossing the vast space, gathering to travel down south. Leopold's eyes smiled.

We'll meet you there. You must teach Louisa how to weave.

The waters closed.

Speedy, translucent meanders tricked the eyes into thinking they were a stationary, solid green mass. Dark patches kept reflecting small lightnings where a sudden beam of sun touched the waves in fragments, like slivers of a broken looking glass.

Rainbow scales of playful trout glistened under the surface. First colored leaves got caught in the stream. They twirled on quick waves like a colorful regatta.

Autumn was coming soon that year. Winter will be long and harsh.

www.ingramcontent.com/pod-product-compliance
Lightning Source LLC
Chambersburg PA
CBHW021445070526
44577CB00002B/265